Goal Processes in Music Therapy Practice

GOAL PROCESSES in MUSIC THERAPY PRACTICE

Grace Thompson

Foreword by Helen Shoemark
Illustrations by Ellen Waite

Jessica Kingsley Publishers
London and Philadelphia

First published in Great Britain in 2022 by Jessica Kingsley Publishers
An imprint of Hodder & Stoughton Ltd
An Hachette Company

1

A CIP catalogue record for this title is available from the
British Library and the Library of Congress

ISBN 978 1 78775 608 3
eISBN 978 1 78775 609 0

Printed and bound in the United States by Integrated Books International

Jessica Kingsley Publishers' policy is to use papers that are natural, renewable and recyclable
products and made from wood grown in sustainable forests. The logging and manufacturing
processes are expected to conform to the environmental regulations of the country of origin.

Jessica Kingsley Publishers
Carmelite House
50 Victoria Embankment
London EC4Y 0DZ

www.jkp.com

To the music therapy students at the University of Melbourne who were not content with the answer 'it depends'.

Contents

Foreword

The invitation to write the foreword for *Goal Processes in Music Therapy Practice* came in a gracious email from Grace Thompson, in which she recalled an early experience as a student in my class. Grace noted that my repeated question 'Why?' on unexplained statements in her assignments contributed to emerging skills to think critically. Fast-forward nearly 30 years, to this book in which Grace uses her honed skills to seek, interpret and produce a meaningful narrative to explain why we do what we do and how it propels the profession of music therapy forward. Grace has a fine international reputation for valuing and sharing the lived experience of individuals and families she has served as clinician and researcher. She brings this together with her capacity to structure new information to help us make sense of those things we know or thought we knew, and bring a new sense of what we need to know.

In my first job as a music therapist, I was particularly proud of my newly honed skills in writing goals for the students in the school. Having nice, neat goals was very pleasing to that part of my brain that said if you can write it, you can do it. But, of course, life is not so tidy. What about the clients who did not fit into the tidy domains I'd established or that the school valued? What about that gut feeling that once in the music room, we were doing something much more than the goals written on the page? This book supports the work that each therapist needs to do as they move beyond their entry-level learning and inhabit their full capacity to meet the needs of their clients. The fundamental remit of the music therapist is to always prepare, anticipate, participate, promote, witness, and document change in clients. It could be tempting to dismiss goal writing as rudimentary or selectively useful, to suggest that it does not warrant attention or that it is suitable only for some kinds of work. But all are disputable assumptions. Rigorous examination and reconsideration of foundational aspects of practice serve to sustain excellence in practice. This book exemplifies the benefits of just such a process.

At the heart of the book, Grace uses a significant grounded theory study she undertook across several countries where music therapy is well established. The questions she asked each of the 45 participants are rooted in Grace's understanding of what is needed now in the profession. The essence of the book is both practice-near and experience-near (Froggett & Briggs, 2012; Geertz, 1974), utilizing the familiar and accessible language of the 45 study participants to develop the key constructs within the theory. The addition of reflexive questions and worksheets allows you as the reader to engage in your own reflexive consideration of your own practice.

At first glance, it is unsurprising to find therapist, client, and context as the organizing forces of the client-in-context theory. But Grace uses the grounded theory to dismantle these concepts into a fresh reality, exemplified by the simple statement in Chapter 3 that 'therapy must always have a purpose'. The central concept of *therapeutic focus* allows you the autonomy to interpret the detail and implementation, respecting the full potential of each person's work whether it is relational, process or outcomes oriented. Grace encourages you to explore the new framework to enhance the rigor of your thinking, interpretations of your clients' autonomy, your own openness, the moderating influence of the real-world context in which the work occurs. These primary elements in the client-in-context theory shake loose implicit aspects to revitalize and create currency in your clinical work.

It is no longer possible to talk about the context of therapy without situating it in ecological systems of culture (Shoemark & Ettenberger, 2020). This book provides an evident cultural lens drawing connections from wide geo-political structures in towards the intimate levels of how music therapy is enacted in time and place. The book will support you in moving beyond the generic ideal of 'music therapy can…' to the culturally specific formation of therapist-in-context.

As we begin to truly re-evaluate the power dynamics in therapeutic relationships, perhaps the strongest contribution of the client-in-context theory is that it celebrates the mutuality and agency of the client inclusive of all levels of capacity, to elevate the client's place in communication and decisions about the role music plays in their life.

Amidst the uncertainty of the COVID pandemic, this book calmly creates a narrative which draws us safely from a familiar certainty to an innovative restructuring of goal setting and writing. In an era when person-centred constructs are cutting through to partner with financial rationalization, it is clear that goal setting and writing will remain a persistent tenet of music therapy services into the future. Achieving a fresh clarity will support advocacy for the role of music in our clients' lives.

Helen Shoemark
Associate Professor of Music Therapy
Temple University, Philadelphia, USA

REFERENCES

Froggett, L. & Briggs, S. (2012). Practice-near and practice-distant methods in human services research. *Journal of Research Practice 8*(2), Article M9. Accessed on 3/11/2021 at http://jrp.icaap.org/index.php/jrp/article/view/318/276

Geertz, C. (1974). From the native's point of view: On the nature of anthropological understanding. *Bulletin of the American Academy of Arts and Sciences 28*(1), 26–45. Accessed on 3/11/2021 at http://hypergeertz.jku.at/GeertzTexts/Natives_Point.htm

Shoemark, H. & Ettenberger, M. (2020). *Music Therapy in Neonatal Intensive Care: Influences of Culture.* New Braunfels, TX: Barcelona Publishers.

Acknowledgements

Undertaking a major piece of writing has made me acutely aware of the resources and support from others that I am fortunate to have. None of this would have been possible as an individual endeavour, as nothing ever is in this world. We are all dependent on others, our culture, our society, and the lands we inhabit. My loving partner, Grant, has walked every step of this project with me, both physically and emotionally. We travelled together for three months to collect the interview data that forms the foundation of this work. To have Grant's support is an incredible privilege for which I am truly thankful.

As a child of a migrant family who did not speak English when they arrived in Australia, education was highly valued and academic achievement was celebrated. I can remember my mum, Cathy, reading to me, singing with me, checking my spelling, and celebrating exam results. Mum would read my essay drafts in high school, and with her keen eye, she would pick up spelling and grammatical errors and strive for excellence. She always made me feel that I could succeed academically and created space for me to focus on my music and my studies. There must be so many more contributions to my education, but exactly how it all came to be is quite mysterious to me. The intersecting influences from my family, community, friends, schoolteachers, peers, and music teachers have provided me with the resources to forge ahead. I am both grateful and humbled to have these resources around me when so many inequities still exist in our society.

My colleagues and students at the University of Melbourne are also an integral part of this book. Special thanks to my mentor and friend, Kat Skewes McFerran, for her generosity and encouragement. When I first started teaching at the university, I was fortunate to work alongside Kat and observe her engaging approach with students; I have been inspired ever since. Through working together to develop case-based learning approaches, Kat guided me to deepen my understanding of curriculum design to support students to become critical thinkers. Kat reviewed a draft of this book and provided insightful feedback that helped to shape this final version for which I am incredibly grateful.

Kim Dunphy was a dance movement therapist at the University of Melbourne with expertise in assessment practices. Kim was enthusiastic about my research and grounded theory, and saw immediate application to other creative arts therapy disciplines. Kim incorporated my research publication in her course content and provided valuable feedback around ways to improve the scaffolding of student learning. These conversations with Kim led me to develop the materials in Chapters 8 and 9. Sadly, Kim passed away while I was working on this manuscript, and I wish I were able to thank her in person for helping me to complete this work.

To the students I have had the privilege to teach since 2010, thank you for all the questions you have asked, all the times you asked 'why', and all the times you wanted more information. As happens in excellent learning cultures, we have mutually gained knowledge that has shaped our understanding and the content of subsequent classes. You are all the inspiration for this book, and I hope that this resource will be a useful part of your reflexivity toolkit. Music therapy is an amazing profession, and music therapy students are truly a joy to teach.

To my music therapy colleagues, particularly Bronte Arns and the Giant Steps Music Therapy Team in Sydney, thank you for your comments, encouragement, and suggestions. To be able to 'road test' the concepts with you has helped to refine the worksheets and reflective prompts throughout this book.

Thank you to the University of Melbourne for supporting this research as part of a teaching and learning special project for six months. The freedom to contemplate, discuss, critique, and reflect is an incredible opportunity and one that few people have the support to undertake. It is a joy to work with inspiring colleagues at the Faculty of Fine Arts and Music, the then Dean Barry Conyngham and the Music Therapy team in particular.

Thank you to the 45 music therapists who participated in the research interviews that have not only informed the grounded theory research but also provided gems of insight that have been interwoven into the chapters. Your openness, whole-hearted dialogue, and willingness to share and debate during the interviews are greatly appreciated and will always be remembered warmly. Thank you to Ellen Waite for the beautiful illustrations and worksheets.

I acknowledge the traditional owners of the unceded land on which this manuscript was written, the people of the Kulin nations. I pay my respects to their Elders, past and present.

PART 1

SETTING THE SCENE

CHAPTER 1

Introduction

Do I need to write a goal?

The question 'Do I need to write a goal?' may feel controversial for music therapists and creative arts therapists for a variety of reasons. Some might say, 'Of course, goals are essential', and therefore be unsure why the question needs to be asked in the first place. Others might say, 'It depends', because they consider that it is the context within which they work that determines their approach. Therefore, the way each person answers this question will vary according to numerous factors, including their years of experience (or stage of training), geographical location, and area of specialization to name just a few.

This book is essentially an elaboration of what 'it depends' means for goal-writing approaches and processes. It is also informed by my belief that goals are a central part of the broader therapy process. As a teacher and supervisor, I have been curious about why there are limited resources describing how music therapists go about identifying and writing goals. To address this gap, I conducted a grounded theory research project (Thompson, 2020) where I interviewed 45 music therapists from nine different countries and invited them to describe: (1) their approach to goals/aims within their own music therapy practice, (2) what they consider to be the main factors that influence their approach to goals/aims, and (3) what they consider to be important when supporting students to understand goals/aims in music therapy. This book is therefore centred around the result-ant theory from that research project, and the rich descriptions of practice captured during approximately 30 hours of interviews and focus group discussions. In addition, I will also synthesize and discuss key pieces of literature in music therapy, creative arts therapies, and therapy more generally to set the scene for the resultant theory and offer guidance for how to apply this literature and theory to therapy practice.

Before diving deeper into the theory that emerged, I'd like to share what I consider to be two provocative quotes from the research participants about their approach to goals in music therapy. To set the scene, all of the interviewees[1] had practice experience ranging from 5 to 42 years and were either teachers in music therapy train-ing courses, supervisors, or both. For this theory-building research project, I wanted to hear perspectives from therapists who had spent considerable time reflecting on these practice issues. These inform-ants were purposively selected as having a high level of expertise and experience in conveying their practice to students or junior col-leagues. Here are two excerpts that highlight the complexity involved in answering the question 'Do I need to write a goal?'

> If I think of my work in palliative care... Well, there is no goal. I mean there is a goal of being there with that person in that moment. That's it. There is no positive progression because...these are the last hours of the [person's life]. So what is the goal in that extreme situation? Maybe the goal is just saying 'We are here, I am listening, what can be done together?' And that openness, I think, somehow music has this strange capacity of reopening the listening process and awareness of the present moment.

Domenico, music therapist working with
people receiving palliative care in Italy

---

1   Pseudonyms are used to refer to the interview participants throughout this book.

Domenico seems to consider that a 'goal' must indicate progression towards an objectively measurable improvement of some sort. He suggests this is not relevant to his work in palliative care settings, yet he also believes that the music therapy sessions are meaningful and important to the people he works with.

> I would get an IEP goal [from the school] that said, 'By the end of the year, this child will be able to give a two-step command or follow a two-step command.' So I would say [to myself], 'Okay, well, I'll turn that into a stop-start activity [in music therapy].' But I always, I knew early on that...I was just playing a game. I was just...it didn't necessarily ever translate into any of my sessions... And now I see it as an art. You know, I have this time-oriented music thing happening, and I can't stop what's happening [in the music]... I was trying to find creative ways to...try to integrate all these worlds, in the context of this person I'm with. If it was a perfect world, and I didn't have to worry about the context of the healthcare facilities and what their expectations are, you know, I could very easily, for myself, remain within a music-centred goal perspective.

Jake, reflecting on his early work in
special education in the USA

In the early days of his career, Jake describes struggling with a clash between what he considered most valuable about music experiences and the expectations from his employer for how music therapy should be considered alongside the IEP[2] goal and applied in the special school setting. Back then, he seemed unsure about how to navigate this clash, and it seems that he had his own covert goals for music therapy that he believed were more relevant and meaningful to the students at this school.

These two interview excerpts typify the vulnerability that many of the participants in the research project expressed. At times, interviewees were not quite sure how to explain their approach to goal

---

2   IEP is a term used in special education meaning 'individual education plan', which documents each student's goals and the supports needed to achieve them.

processes within their work, and yet they did have a clear sense of their practice and values. The way the interviewees described centring the needs of the people they work with to provide an attuned and therapeutic space was also incredibly touching.

It might seem strange to highlight these vulnerable and tentative statements about practice. Within the full interviews, our conversations dug further into the details, and these will be shared throughout the book. The subsequent analysis provides a theoretical framework to guide learning and reflective practice that aims to move beyond specific training models or geographical contextual factors and instead describe a shared essence of music therapy practice. It is my hope that this theory is also relevant to other creative arts therapy disciplines.

These experienced practitioners also conveyed that being flexible and responsive in goal-writing processes was most important. Many participants expressed that this *way of being* was more important than simply focusing on the technical aspect of how to *write* a goal, and more useful than providing lists of topics/domains that might be appropriate for people with various conditions. I have therefore used extensive quotes and composite case examples that combine several perspectives to help convey the importance of flexibility and responsiveness to music therapy students and new graduates in particular.

Sitting alongside this responsive way of being, the participants further emphasized the weight of ethical responsibility they feel during goal processes. In my own reflections on previous literature, this ethical perspective is often underestimated in favour of more functional descriptions of how to write a goal. The distinction between goal *writing* and goal *processes* is important to be aware of while engaging with the upcoming chapters. Goal processes refer to the different actions and behaviours that therapists and the people they work with undertake to identify a focus for the therapy (Cooper & Law, 2018).

GOALS IN THE CONTEXT OF PROFESSIONAL STANDARDS OF PRACTICE

Music therapists working in countries where there is a professional association generally must agree to abide by a Code of Ethics and/ or a Standards of Practice to achieve and maintain accreditation. These documents often define and operationalize, to some degree, the expectations of professional practice. Standards of Practice are broad-based documents intended to guide the spectrum of possible practice, and therefore they are important in shaping the direction of the profession.

To take an example from my own country, the Australian Music Therapy Association defines seven key 'professional procedures', which are: (1) Accepting referrals, (2) Assessment, (3) Planning, (4) Implementation, (5) Documentation, (6) Evaluation, and (7) Termination (Australian Music Therapy Association, 2021, p.16). Each of these procedures is elaborated upon further within the Standards of Practice document, but we can start to build an impression of music therapy practice and professional identity straight away by considering these procedures. Within this Australian example, music therapy begins with a person or organization who approaches a music therapist with a reason they wish to engage, then flows through various stages of 'work' together, and eventually to a time where the music therapist and the individual or group will part ways. Procedures related to goals are further outlined under 'planning' for music therapy sessions as follows.

Australian Music Therapy Association Standards of Practice
Professional Procedure: Planning

Item 3.2. The music therapy program is expressed as goals/ aims; objectives; purposes or intentions. These may vary according to the philosophy of the facility, the needs of the

Client/s and the philosophical orientation of the Registered Music Therapist (RMT).

Item 3.3. In some situations, the aims may unfold as the program progresses, and may be influenced by the changing needs of the Client, and the evolving nature of the therapy. They may also relate to exploring the most effective means of communicating or interacting with Client/s and may involve a trial of differing music therapy methods and approaches.

Item 3.4. In some situations, aims are difficult to formulate because the RMT may be meeting the Client for the first and only time. In approaching the Client to provide a one-off music therapy session, the RMT may be guided by intentions for the interaction and through information gathered by members of the treating team, referrers, and/or family members.

Extract from 2021 document, page 17

Reflecting on these procedures for planning from my own Association, I believe this document reflects the pragmatic approach to Australian music therapy practice in which my knowledge is situated. As described in the box above, the Australian Association considers there are a variety of ways to articulate music therapy practice, from goals and objectives to purposes and intentions. There is also an acknowledgement that the sometimes short-term and fluid nature of music therapy practice creates potential challenges for communicating the aim of music therapy sessions.

Although reviewing documents from every country with a professional association for music therapy is beyond the scope of this chapter, I will give two further examples from English-speaking countries with large populations of qualified music therapists: the United States of America and the United Kingdom. Similar to Australia, in the USA there is an overall procedure for practice outlined: (1) referral and acceptance, (2) assessment, (3) treatment planning,

(4) implementation, (5) documentation, and (6) termination. However, the terminology used implies a more medical orientation, as suggested through the inclusion of descriptors such as 'clinical practice' and 'treatment planning'. Within the process of 'treatment planning', specifications for goals and objectives are briefly elaborated and reproduced below (American Music Therapy Association, 2015).

American Music Therapy Association Standards of Clinical Practice
Standard: Treatment Planning

Item 3. The Music Therapist will develop an individualized treatment plan based upon the music therapy assessment, the client's prognosis, and applicable information from other disciplines and sources. The client will participate in program plan development when appropriate. The music therapy program plan will be designed to:

Item 3.4 Contain goals that focus on assessed needs and strengths of the client. Goals are a projected outcome of a treatment plan. Goals are often stated in broad terms, as opposed to objectives which are stated more specifically.

Item 3.5 Contain objectives which are operationally defined for achieving the stated goals within estimated time frames. An objective is one of a series of progressive accomplishments leading toward goal attainment; may include conditions under which the expected outcome occurs.

Extract taken from American Music Therapy
Association website © 2015

The American description of goals and objectives is more concrete and therefore less fluid or pragmatic. As expressed in the 2015 document, the music therapy program plan *will* contain both goals and objectives, and goals are expected to be a *projected outcome* of the music therapy sessions. This construction of the Standards of Practice positions music therapy more directly as a treatment, where a client can expect a clear and delineated outcome will be articulated. No further guidance is offered within this document regarding how the music therapist might establish these goals and objectives beyond the precursor of an assessment. There is an assumption perhaps that goals and objectives will logically follow from such an assessment.

In contrast, practising music therapists in the UK are required to be registered with the Health and Care Professions Council (HCPC) and abide by the Standards of Proficiency for Arts Therapists (Health and Care Professions Council, 2018). The HCPC document is much broader and less prescriptive than those from Australia and the USA, highlighting the different ways therapy practice can be viewed around the world. Goal processes within the HCPC Standards are alluded to under broader items such as 'effective communication', 'appropriate work', 'quality of practice', 'professional knowledge base', and 'practice knowledge and skills' as follows.

Health and Care Professions Council Standards of Proficiency for Arts Therapists

Item 8. Be able to communicate effectively
    8.9 be able to explain the nature, purpose and techniques of therapy to service users and carers
Item 9. Be able to work appropriately with others
    9.3 understand the need to engage service users and carers in planning and evaluating diagnostics and assessment outcomes to meet their needs and goals
Item 12. Be able to assure the quality of their practice
    12.6 be able to evaluate intervention plans using recognised outcome measures and revise the plans as necessary in conjunction with the service user
    12.7 recognise the need to monitor and evaluate the quality

of practice and the value of contributing to the generation of data for quality assurance and improvement programmes

Item 13. Understand the key concepts of the knowledge base relevant to their profession

13.11 be able to employ a coherent approach to the therapeutic process

Item 14. Be able to draw on appropriate knowledge and skills to inform practice

14.2 be able to work with service users both to define a clear end for the therapy, and to evaluate the therapy's strengths, benefits and limitations

14.3 be able to formulate specific and appropriate management plans including the setting of timescales

Extract from 2018 document

These three examples of practice standards document similarly intend to outline the broad process a therapist might follow. The nuances in expression of the function and nature of goal processes (or lack thereof in the case of the HCPC document) suggest that practice in each location would differ in important ways. These are only three examples; the equivalent documents published by each professional association for music therapy around the world may similarly convey the underlying approach to practice in each context.

Invitation to reflexivity: Are you accredited or registered with a professional association? What, if any, professional standards for goal processes are published by the association to which you belong? Do you feel these documents reflect your practice?

PROTOCOLS VERSUS PROCESSES

A hallmark of the teaching team at the University of Melbourne is to qualify every answer to practice-based questions with the statement 'it depends'. My students often roll their eyes when the qualifier 'it depends' is uttered, and one cohort even had the saying printed on their graduation T-shirts! While the students understand that context is important, some are also frustrated by the lack of certainty and guidance they perceive in this qualified answer. In other words, many seem to want a protocol for every situation.

In my other role as a supervisor of qualified music therapists, my supervisees generally see the value and importance of unpacking the context of their work to reflect on what has taken place and consider further possibilities. As we mature as therapists, we become (a little) better at sitting with uncertainty and constructing our approach or framework to practice. The process that continually unfolds and flows through the dynamic interactions between music therapists and the people we work with are more accepted and acknowledged.

As a teacher and supervisor, I believe that protocols, guidelines, or standards of practice are not an adequate substitute for theory. Theory can be applied, extended, and challenged. Protocols and standards cannot, even when these documents attempt to allow for flexibility. The next chapter provides a critical reflection on the literature related to goals in therapy, and the subsequent research I undertook.

CLARIFYING TERMS

Before ending this chapter, I would like to clarify the terminology I will adopt throughout this book. When referring to the people music therapists work with, there are various terms and conventions that individuals and organizations prefer. The people we work with might be referred to as participants, clients, patients, residents, students, service users, and consumers, to name a few. Scholars and practitioners have long debated the power connotations implied within these terms. Carl Rogers, one of the innovators of humanistic psychology, rejected the term 'patient' in favour of 'client' in an effort to distinguish humanist approaches from the prevailing medical model that positioned the therapist as the expert in diagnosis and treatment (Elkins, 2009; Rogers, 1951). Personally, I generally feel comfortable with the term 'client' as for me it conveys a sense that there can be a collaborative agreement or contract between people. I also admit that I like the grammatical economy of this term. However, others, such as Katrina McFerran (McFerran, 2021), argue that the pragmatic use of these collective terms still positions the people we work with as 'others', as if they are a homogenous group of people needing help which dangerously strips away our understanding of each individual's diversity and personhood.

Given that the terms therapists use in their workplaces are informed by the context, writing a book that invites reflections on practice across contexts makes it challenging to select a consensus term. Therefore, I encourage readers to think of 'the person/s they work with' throughout the following chapters. I have opted to predominantly use the terms 'person' and 'persons' to signal that our work as music therapists is always relational, and that individuals' circumstances are centred and respected. There are, however, times where the term 'client' will be used when I need to refer to the language used within published reports and documents.

REFERENCES

American Music Therapy Association (2015). *Standards of Clinical Practice*. Accessed on 3/11/2021 at www.musictherapy.org/about/standards

Australian Music Therapy Association (2021). Code of Ethics. Australian Music Therapy Association. Accessed on 12/11/2021 at www.austmta.org.au/public/151/files/Website%20general/Code%20of%20Ethics%202021.pdf

Cooper, M. & Law, D. (2018). Introduction. In M. Cooper & D. Law (eds), *Working with Goals in Psychotherapy and Counselling*. Oxford: Oxford University Press.

Elkins, D.N. (2009). The medical model in psychotherapy: Its limitations and failures. *Journal of Humanistic Psychology 49*(1), 66–84. Accessed on 3/11/2021 at https://doi.org/10.1177/0022167807307901

Health and Care Professions Council (2018). *The standards of proficiency for arts therapists*. HCPC. Accessed on 31/01/2022 at www.hcpc-uk.org/standards/standards-of-proficiency/arts-therapists

McFerran, K.S. (2021). Reconsidering the dominant narratives of the music therapy profession for the future. *Canadian Journal of Music Therapy, 27*, 21–34.

Rogers, C.R. (1951) *Client-Centered Therapy*. Boston, MA: Houghton Mifflin.

Thompson, G.A. (2020). A grounded theory of music therapists' approach to goal processes within their clinical practice. *The Arts in Psychotherapy 70*. Accessed on 3/11/2021 at https://doi.org/https://doi.org/10.1016/j.aip.2020.101680

CHAPTER 2

Reflections on literature

Like all therapists, music therapists need to articulate why they are doing what they are doing. The therapeutic goal is a succinct yet powerful way to communicate many aspects of therapy. The goal can indicate what is valued in the process, beliefs about health and prognosis, and beliefs about the agency of the people we are working with in their own health trajectory. Identifying and writing goals is a nuanced and complex undertaking that requires therapists to do more than write clearly. The goal must be relevant, meaningful, motivating, and ethical. The goal should have integrity; by this, I mean that the therapist and person they are working with share a level of agreement (consent or assent) about the direction and focus. Goals can therefore be viewed as central to our communication of the therapy process and our professionalism.

The therapist's employment context also impacts the goal process. Some settings or funding arrangements require goals to be articulated before the therapy commences in earnest, typically following a formal assessment or consultation period of some kind. Other work contexts are open to a more emergent approach to ascertaining the goal for therapy or consider that a broad statement of purpose is sufficient. Understanding how goal processes flow through to the way we work with people can help to deepen or even expand our scope of practice.

To give an example of how the process we undertake can have significant impacts on practice, I invite you to engage in this description that comes from outside of the therapy professions. In this interview, Lee Child, author of the Jack Reacher fiction books, describes his creative writing process for determining the plot lines of his novels:

> I work in a, what we call 'seat of the pants' [approach]. You know, there's two types of writers in this genre: what they call the 'plotters' and the 'pansters'. And I'm the panster. I'm the king of the pansters! I have no clue what's going to happen in the next paragraph let alone the end of the book. Because to me, the thing that really captures my interest is not necessarily completing a novel, it's telling myself the story. I'm just fascinated by story. And so if I planned it out, even to any degree, even if it was just one sheet of scribbled notes, I would know the story and I would no longer be interested in it. I'd be ready for the next story. So, it's really important to me that I don't know what's going to happen. I wanna let the story, the book, evolve organically and naturally. And it's an insecure way to do it. You feel like it's a high-wire and you could fall off at any point and go nowhere. But actually, I find it so helpful because you've got total liberty to go off in any direction. If something that you've just written strikes you as bearing new possibilities, you can just head in that direction. Whereas I think if you had an outline, you would feel straitjacketed by it. You would feel reluctant to depart from it because then the outline is meaningless. (Kanowski, 2018)

When I listened to this interview, it struck me that this binary of being a 'plotter' or a 'panster' has some similarities to what Ken Bruscia (2014) describes as 'outcome-oriented' and 'process-oriented' approaches in music therapy. Within an 'outcome-oriented strategy', the therapist is described as taking a more directive stance in order to 'induce targeted change in the client' (p.176). Specific goals are formulated early on to address a problem that has been pre-identified in a formal assessment process. An example of an outcome-oriented strategy is Suzanne Hanser's 'data-based model' (Hanser, 2018, p.42) that advocates for an evidence-based approach to music therapy. Hanser considers that systematic information gathering must be an essential part of practice, and the data collection process must be clearly aligned with the person's music therapy goals and objectives.

By contrast, Bruscia proposes that therapists working within an 'experience-oriented strategy' often begin with only a preliminary understanding of the individual's needs or reasons for coming to therapy. The therapeutic goals become clearer as the process dynamically unfolds, with the therapist described as taking a more collaborative stance in relation to the person they are working with. Bruscia further clarifies that 'one of the differences between outcome-oriented and experience-oriented strategies is that the former most often begins with pre-established goals, whereas the latter most often begins with a pre-established model or method' (p.180).

While Bruscia's binary can be helpful to understand differences in approaches, there is a problematic dichotomy created because 'outcome' is positioned as distinct from 'process'. To further explain, time and again I have dialogued with students who read this definition and say something along the lines of: 'Well, my employer/client is going to want an outcome...so I'll work in an "outcome-oriented" way.' The assumption of the novice therapist is that there won't be a clear outcome in an experience-oriented approach, which is an unfortunate consequence of Bruscia's choice of terms.

If therapists focus predominantly on writing goals that have objective and observable outcomes, we run the risk of shaping practice in one direction or, worse, leaving future therapists who wish to align with experience-oriented approaches gravely under-equipped. Several of the research participants reflected on the notion of outcome compared with process and highlighted similar concerns, exemplified in the statements below.

I think the word 'outcome' is interesting because many people think about effect. But everything has an outcome, if you like it or not.

Anita from Norway

> We wouldn't do any music therapy if there wasn't any outcome of it. And we wouldn't do music therapy in Norway if we're not process-oriented... We wouldn't say that there is a contradiction between process and outcome.

Lisbeth from Norway

The language we use to describe our work is vital, and therefore it is problematic to consider 'outcomes' as only relevant to specific frameworks or contexts. Taking an example from outside the field of music therapy, psychotherapists and counsellors Cooper and Law (2018) make it clear that outcome-oriented goals are central to their emergent and collaborative practice approach. They describe the case of Gita, who through engaging in active discussions about her personal goals with her therapist, revealed the 'complex, subtle, and dialogical process, in which collaboratively-agreed goals can provide focus and direction to the therapeutic work. Gita's goals give her hope, and also a sense of direction and purpose. They support Gita to move towards her future' (Cooper & Law, 2018, p.2). The goal process within Cooper and Law's emergent approach sounds vibrant and active, and the sense of working towards an outcome is not lost. Given that many professional standards of practice describe the need for goals/aims/objectives, we need a more nuanced understanding of how to articulate what is happening in music therapy practice.

Ken Aigen (2014) also describes two polar perspectives on music therapy practice, but instead links the issues with identity to a more theoretical genesis. While Aigen acknowledges that presenting a dichotomy neglects representing the diversity within the profession, he observes that two dominant identities are nonetheless present: the music therapist as medical professional and the music therapist as psychotherapist (p.17). Aigen depicts the music therapist as medical professional as someone who uses treatment protocols and focuses on observable and measurable outcomes that are clearly articulated in goals and objectives. By contrast, the music therapist as psychotherapist is depicted as placing more emphasis on client empowerment and agency, and as such goals may be less formally expressed. Aigen's depiction suggests that the therapist's values, beliefs, and theoretical influences are the key drivers of their therapy practice.

Randi Rolvsjord (2015) takes a different view by highlighting that the resources and contributions of the people we work with play a crucial role in determining the focus and approach of therapy. The way the therapist engages with the person's resources could also be seen as another type of binary. The therapist might view the person they are working with more from an illness model and seek to address deficits related to their condition, or more from a social model by considering their strengths and the resources they bring to the therapy context (Rolvsjord, 2010). Goals that flow from the illness model might be more likely to result from a formal assessment and seek to address predetermined outcomes. Goals that flow from what Rolvsjord has termed a 'resource-oriented model' might take various creative forms and are determined in collaboration with the person.

As a music therapy educator and supervisor, I noticed that much of the music therapy literature focuses on *writing* goals more so than the manner of *identifying* goals. Further, the literature describing goal-writing techniques tends to privilege a medical or behavioural stance. This stance is evident when authors advocate for therapist-constructed goals that have observable and often non-musical outcomes, and that are written immediately following formal assessments (Hanser, 2018). For students and supervisees, learning about writing goals solely within the context of a medical stance risks fostering a narrow focus on illness, pathology, and elimination of problems. Moreover, privileging one stance does not authentically speak to the breadth of music therapy practice.

Other authors have similar concerns about centring a medically dominant perspective of music therapy. Brian Abrams (Abrams *et al.*, 2016) proposes that music therapists should view music as a domain of health in and of itself. Therefore, health goals can (or must) be expressed as *musical* goals. Abrams acknowledges the language and advocacy challenges of boldly embracing this position, explaining that:

> what we're grappling with is the new territory of trying to find that cohesive language that's legitimate in healthcare contexts, but also is authentic and true to what we all *really* do with our clients and experience...and hopefully come to a more solid sense of [a] clinical-musical-language that can really speak to our goals. (Abrams *et al.*, 2016)

These concerns regarding the pressure music therapists might experience to frame their work to meet the needs of the medical model have relevance for all creative arts therapists. The challenge of authentically conveying our practice through goals also resonates with the provocation from Jake in Chapter 1, where he seemed to have his own covert goals that better aligned with his actual practice compared with the official (and non-musical) goals documented for the employer.

GOALS AND THE POLITICS OF HEALTH SYSTEMS

Meeting the expectations of the people we work with, employers, and funders is important. Alongside this, we also need to consider the possible limitations that health systems can place on creative arts therapy practice which can stifle professional growth and development. For example, therapists informed by humanistic theory that takes a client-centred approach tend to emphasize 'being' over 'doing' (Abrams, 2015). Along a similar vein, psychoanalytic theories emphasize the importance of unconscious mechanisms, where the client and therapist journey together to construct meaning and find a shared path forward (Cooper & Law, 2018). More recently, an 'extended humanism' has been proposed by Ansdell and Stige (2018) which acknowledges the importance of performing the self in community, where 'an ecology of action and interaction' takes place (p.6). For these therapists, writing predetermined goals that measure observable behaviour change must feel like a poor match. Just like Lee Child's 'plotter', goals rigidly set at the commencement of therapy following an assessment could make both therapist and client feel 'straitjacketed' and reluctant to depart from their plan. Indeed, grappling with the process is considered by some to be an essential part of therapy (Bruschweiler-Stern *et al.*, 2010). We need an expanded and more nuanced understanding of goal practices in order to better articulate both the outcomes and process of different approaches to therapy.

Policy and funding for healthcare vary greatly around the world, and often these frameworks evolve in response to social movements and changing social values. Therapists will always need to be responsive to the context and systems they find themselves working within, but in situations where employer expectations do not align with the therapist's approach to practice, tensions are likely to develop. Despite the challenges, practitioners have reported finding ways to genuinely convey and advocate for the distinct focus of creative arts therapies in addressing people's health and wellbeing needs. The following two examples of policy changes in Australia and the United Kingdom illustrate some of the drawbacks and opportunities.

Australian example

The National Disability and Insurance Scheme (NDIS) is a funding model for disability services introduced by the Australian Government in 2016. The philosophy of the scheme aspires to put disabled people, referred to as 'participants', in control of their lives through engaging in a planning process prior to engaging with therapists and service providers. This plan must outline the goals they want to achieve in the upcoming year (NDIS, 2019), and these goals must always be related to the participant's functional capacity, defined as their ability to carry out tasks and actions involved in different areas of life such as home, school, work and the community (NDIS, 2021).

However, the participants do not have complete free choice about the services they can receive, as all plans need to be deemed 'reasonable and necessary'. Even though music therapy is an eligible service within the scheme, it does not mean that each request for music therapy will be accepted. Approval depends on whether music therapy is justified and aligned with the participant's functional goals (Lee *et al.*, 2018). Similar to the concerns raised earlier (Abrams *et al.*, 2016), by privileging a focus on predetermined functional goals, the scheme risks alienating therapists whose approach is more collaborative and emergent. While some therapists may relent and adhere to the focus on functional goals, others may seek to subvert the system and inauthentically promote their work in a narrow way. Expanding our skills in goal writing may help therapists to advocate for a broader scope of practice and increased participant choice and control over their therapy services.

United Kingdom example

The National Health Service (NHS) in the United Kingdom introduced a significant policy change known as the tariff-based model. The tariff-based model funds time-limited therapy in various services, and goals must be established from the beginning to enable evaluation of outcomes (Cooper & Law, 2018). While some critics initially viewed the model as being singularly concerned with cost-effectiveness, proponents highlighted that this approach is favourably aligned with the ethics of recovery models and client choice. Viewed from a recovery model perspective, 'a goal-oriented approach puts the client's own, explicitly stated agenda at the heart of the therapeutic process' (Cooper & Law, 2018, p.6). A research project evaluated the impact of this change on the work of arts psychotherapists employed by the NHS in mental health services (Havsteen-Franklin *et al.*, 2017). Previously, the therapists took an open-ended approach focused on prevention and ongoing support to clients with severe mental illnesses. The new time-limited model's philosophy required them to focus exclusively on the treatment of symptoms. Therapists were initially concerned that focusing on symptom reduction would lead to poorer outcomes and less support for clients. However, clients described distinct benefits of engaging with arts psychotherapies within this time-limited funding model as providing important opportunities to come to terms with overwhelming emotions and to feel safe with others. Rather than arts psychotherapies being at risk of becoming irrelevant in the system, clients instead considered these services to be essential within the new approach (Havsteen-Franklin *et al.*, 2017).

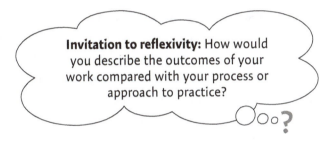

Invitation to reflexivity: How would you describe the outcomes of your work compared with your process or approach to practice?

GOALS AND FRAMEWORKS FOR PRACTICE

So far, I have canvassed various influences on goal writing, including professional guidelines for practice, descriptions of practice strategies, therapists' role identity, and government funding models. Another influence that is commonly discussed is the therapist's framework for practice. These frameworks often combine theoretical positions with conventions that exist in certain contexts. To delve into some of the ways that goals can be influenced by our frameworks, I have grouped the literature into three broad topics: expert frameworks, collaborative frameworks, and developmental frameworks. These are by no means the only possible practice frameworks, but they usefully highlight some key factors that have a bearing on goals.

Expert frameworks

Music therapists aligned with expert frameworks may describe their work as a 'treatment'. From this stance, music experiences are designed according to protocols that assume a similar effect will result when a music 'stimulus' is provided to people with similar presenting issues (Berger, 2009). Goals and objectives therefore emphasize minimizing specific problems and deficits related to the client's diagnosis (Berger, 2009; Sena Moore & LaGasse, 2018), and are typically written by the therapy team following a formal assessment (Gfeller & Davis, 2008; Hanser, 2018). Outcomes typically need to be objectively measurable and linked to observable behaviours (Berger, 2009; Hanser, 2018; Hardy & LaGasse, 2018).

This framework requires a highly specific style of goal writing that is exemplified by the SMART goal protocol. This protocol originated in the business sector as a way to measure employee performance and productivity (Doran, 1981). Within therapy contexts, the acronym commonly stands for **S**pecific, **M**easurable, **A**chievable, **R**ealistic, and **T**imed goals (Bovend'Eerdt *et al.*, 2009; Hanser, 2018). The intention is to construct goals and objectives that are unambiguous and have a clear means to be evaluated within a defined time frame (Bovend'Eerdt *et al.*, 2009; Gfeller & Davis, 2008; Hanser, 2018; Polen *et al.*, 2017). Objectives may be updated regularly but are commonly established prior to the commencement of treatment in order to plan a systematic intervention that can be independently evaluated (Hanser, 2018).

While each therapist will have their own interpersonal style that may include more participatory and collaborative principles, the expert framework privileges the therapist's specialist knowledge. In certain contexts, this is completely appropriate. For example, a study of occupational therapists and physiotherapists working in stroke rehabilitation settings revealed they had serious concerns about working more collaboratively with their patients, including: concerns for health and safety if patients selected goals that were beyond their current abilities; concerns that the patient would choose to do no therapy and therefore compromise their physical recovery; and perceived loss of their own professional status and influence despite wanting to be more collaborative (Norris & Kilbride, 2014). While the study highlights the complexity of the therapist's relationship with their patients, the findings make it clear that in certain contexts a SMART goal written by the treatment team is highly ethical.

Collaborative frameworks

Music therapists aligned with theories that promote an individual's agency and collaboration in service provision emphasize the importance of each person's culture and sense of their ideal healthy-self as providing the focus or direction in the therapy (Loewy, 2000; Rolvsjord, 2010). Along with therapists informed by humanistic and psychodynamic theories, practitioners who are aligned with community-based and culture-centred approaches could also be included here (Stige, 2002; Stige & Aarø, 2011). For these practitioners, approaches to assessment are typically more holistic and take into account relational and emotional themes that extend beyond the symptoms or impairments associated with a diagnosis or condition. In fact, the term 'assessment' may be avoided altogether, given its association with an expert framework, with alternative terms adopted such as 'hang out period' (Bolger & McFerran, 2013), 'getting a feel for the system' (McFerran & Rickson, 2014) or the therapist actively engaging in 'reflective' and 'ethics-driven' collaborations (Stige & Aarø, 2011). Within this collaborative ethos, the therapist strives to create mutual understanding and 'buy in' to the therapeutic process for all participants (Bolger et al., 2018).

Rather than describing specific goals, therapists working within collaborative frameworks might state the overall intention of their practice, sometimes termed as 'purpose statements' (Abbott, 2020; Polen et al., 2017). For example, music therapists aligned with humanistic tenets have described their work as 'the client and therapist engage[d] in various ways of being, musically, to support self-actualisation' (Abrams, 2015, p.153). Music therapists adopting an advocacy or rights-based approach have defined overall aims of music therapy as offering 'a safe space for clients to musically express their LGBTQ identities openly, embrace differences...acknowledge systemic oppression...and celebrate their individuality and group identities' (Bain *et al.*, 2016). In a similar way, music therapists aligned with social justice principles have opted to describe the overall purpose of their work – for example, 'the use of music therapy approaches in the community to increase social and cultural awareness and bring a sense of societal participation to all concerned' (Vaillancourt, 2012, p.175).

Beyond the profession of music therapy, counsellors and psychotherapists similarly highlight the importance of collaborative frameworks as a way to support basic psychological needs for autonomy, relatedness, and competence (Poulsen *et al.*, 2015). The complex relational dynamics that occur when collaborating to determine the direction or focus of therapy are overtly acknowledged within these frameworks, such as understanding that 'not all clients who come to therapy are able to articulate their goals. Some clients may not feel safe enough to disclose their true goals until they have developed sufficient trust in their therapist' (Cooper & McLeod, 2007, p.137). In contrast, therapists have also described how openly negotiating goals at the start of therapy supported the therapeutic alliance and helped illuminate differences in expectations (McGuire *et al.*, 2016; Odhammar & Carlberg, 2015).

Within this collaborative framework, goals are not viewed as rigid or fixed, but rather can be fluid and approximately point to a desired future outcome (Cooper & Law, 2018; Odhammar & Carlberg, 2015; Poulsen *et al.*, 2015). Therefore, therapists acknowledge that 'recovery can mean different things to different people' (Jacob *et al.*, 2016, p.219), and the person's subjective evaluation of their own outcomes is highly relevant (Martikainen *et al.*, 2002). Collaborating in goal writing can be one way to 'bring all parties more in alignment with what needs to be worked on' (Jacob *et al.*, 2016, p.211) and ensure that goals are expressed in the way the client wishes them to be (Bruschweiler-Stern *et al.*, 2010; McGuire *et al.*, 2016; Tryon & Winograd, 2011).

Developmental frameworks

When working with children and young people, music therapists are often guided by an understanding of child development stages and the environmental and social factors that nurture development over time (Carpente, 2018). Alongside an understanding of developmental stages, music therapy practice with children and young people often takes into account the systems within which we meet the child. Bronfenbrenner (1979) first articulated an ecological framework for human development, highlighting that children cannot be considered in isolation from the people or institutions that directly impact them. Therefore, child development is always affected by family relationships and resources, education institutions, and the community. While an ecological framework can be applied to work with people across the lifespan, there are particular considerations for the way systems might influence goal writing for children and young people.

In school contexts, goal processes are often embedded within the education system. For disabled children, each child typically has an 'individual education plan' established through consultation with the school, family, and other therapy service providers (Hardy & LaGasse, 2018). Goals often focus on maximizing the child's development by addressing needs related to both their diagnosis and the school curriculum (Geretsegger *et al.*, 2015; Kaplan & Steele, 2005). Schools and education boards may require goals and objectives to be expressed in specific and measurable ways in order to keep track of developmental progress (Carpente, 2013, 2018; Hardy & LaGasse, 2018; Jung, 2007; Wallen & Stewart, 2015). There may be an overlap with expert frameworks at these times, since goals are typically determined from a formal assessment prior to the commencement of therapy and laid out in a developmental hierarchy (Hardy & LaGasse, 2018).

Monitoring of outcomes is sometimes very finely graded, as described by 'goal attainment scaling' processes that seek to evaluate the degree to which a goal is achieved over time (Wallen & Stewart, 2015).

By contrast, family-centred and community-based approaches tend to overlap with collaborative frameworks. Drawing again on Bronfenbrenner's (1979) premise that the child's needs cannot be considered in isolation, the music therapist often seeks to collaboratively determine the focus and direction of therapy with the family (Molyneux *et al.*, 2012; Thompson, 2016). The child or young person's developmental needs therefore sit alongside considerations for the needs of the whole family system. Goals might focus specifically on the child's developmental progress, or the quality of the parent–child relationship, or supporting parent self-efficacy and wellbeing, or a combination of these aspects. Negotiating the goals with family members requires sensitivity and compassion. Stine Jacobsen and I noted many challenges in our analysis of collaborative goal-writing approaches within family-centred practice. In particular, the most challenging moments occur when therapists and family members have different levels of insight into how the overall health of the system is impacting the child's development. The process of negotiation and collaboration requires careful facilitation, and so goals might only be broadly expressed initially before becoming more specific and focused over time (Jacobsen & Thompson, 2016).

CONSIDERING REAL-LIFE PROFESSIONAL CHALLENGES

In attempting to highlight the different values, beliefs, theories, and approaches that might inform goal writing in different contexts, it is important to also understand that many music therapists work across multiple contexts simultaneously. It is also common for music therapists to undertake short-term contracts or projects. While a therapist might resonate with a particular approach, working for multiple employers in diverse practice settings will demand flexibility from the therapist. Additionally, social policy and values change over time, which demands that therapists revisit their intentions and values as practitioners (Pickard *et al.*, 2020).

However, no matter the therapist's approach, it seems that goals in some shape or form are a dominant feature of professional practices. A recent survey of music therapists in the USA found that 87% of respondents indicated that writing goals and objectives (or other similar statements) are part of their planning process (Abbott, 2020). In reflecting on the diverse responses from participants in her survey study, Elaine Abbott acknowledges that goal processes need to be flexible to meet the needs of different practice contexts. Abbott recommends that music therapists need to 'become conceptual thinkers who can flexibly respond to philosophical and pragmatic changes within and across clinical settings' (Abbott, 2020, p.185). I very much agree with this statement. It is important then to consider the resources that might assist therapists to achieve this flexibility in a coherent and contained way.

In the next chapter, I will outline the need for a theory, rather than a protocol, for goal process in music therapy. A theory allows for a broad-based understanding to be developed that can be part of the resources a therapist draws upon in their practice. Through this expansion, professional and trainee music therapists can find an alternative to the 'one-size-fits-all' approach that often permeates different models and protocols for how to 'write' a goal. I will then introduce the resultant grounded theory from my research project: the client-in-context.

REFERENCES

Abbott, E.A. (2020). Music therapists' goal and objective writing practices. *Music Therapy Perspectives 38*(2), 178–186. Accessed on 3/11/2021 at https://doi.org/10.1093/mtp/miz018

Abrams, B. (2015). Humanistic Approaches. In B.L. Wheeler (ed.) *Music Therapy Handbook*. New York, NY: Guildford Press.

Abrams, B., Murphy, K., Potvin, N. & Young, L. (2016). MT goals from musical perspective [Audio podcast episode]. In American Music Therapy Association, *AMTA-Pro Podcast Series*. Accessed on 3/11/2021 at http://amtapro.musictherapy. org/?p=1574

Aigen, K. (2014). *The Study of Music Therapy: Current Issues and Concepts*. London and New York, NY: Routledge.

Ansdell, G. & Stige, B. (2018). Can music therapy still be humanist? *Music Therapy Perspectives 36*(2), 175–182.

Bain, C.L., Grzanka, P.R. & Crowe, B.J. (2016). Toward a queer music therapy: The implications of queer theory for radically inclusive music therapy. *The Arts in Psychotherapy 50*, 22–33. Accessed on 31/01/2022 at https://doi.org/10.1016/j. aip.2016.03.004

Berger, D.S. (2009). On developing music therapy goals and objectives. *Voices: A World Forum for Music Therapy 9*(1). Accessed on 3/11/2021 at https://doi. org/10.15845/voices.v9i1.362

Bolger, L. & McFerran, K. (2013). Demonstrating sustainability in the practices of music therapists: Reflections from Bangladesh. *Voices: A World Forum for Music Therapy 13*(2). Accessed on 3/11/2021 at http://dx.doi.org/10.15845/voices.v13i2.715

Bolger, L., McFerran, K.S. & Stige, B. (2018). Hanging out and buying in: Rethinking relationship building to avoid tokenism when striving for collaboration in music therapy. *Music Therapy Perspectives 36*(2), 257–266. Accessed on 3/11/2021 at https://doi.org/10.1093/mtp/miy002

Bovend'Eerdt, T.J., Botell, R.E. & Wade, D.T. (2009). Writing SMART rehabilitation goals and achieving goal attainment scaling: a practical guide. *Clinical Rehabilitation 23*(4), 352–361. Accessed on 3/11/2021 at https://doi. org/10.1177/0269215508101741

Bronfenbrenner, U. (1979). *The Ecology of Human Development: Experiments by Nature and Design*. Cambridge, MA: Harvard University Press.

Bruschweiler-Stern, N.C., Lyons-Ruth, K.C., Morgan, A.C., Nahum, J.P. *et al.* (2010). *Change in Psychotherapy: A Unifying Paradigm*. New York, NY: W.W. Norton & Co.

Bruscia, K.E. (2014). *Defining Music Therapy* (3rd edn). New Braunfels, TX: Barcelona Publishers.

Carpente, J.A. (2013). *The Individual Music-Centered Assessment Profile for Neurodevelopmental Disorders: A Clinical Manual*. Baldwin, NY: Regina Publishers.

Carpente, J.A. (2018). Goal attainment scaling: A method for evaluating progress toward developmentally based music-centered treatment goals for children with autism spectrum disorder. *Music Therapy Perspectives 36*(2), 215–223. Accessed on 3/11/2021 at https://doi.org/https://doi.org/10.1093/mtp/mix021

Cooper, M. & Law, D. (2018). Introduction. In M. Cooper & D. Law (eds) *Working with Goals in Psychotherapy and Counselling*. Oxford: Oxford University Press.

Cooper, M. & McLeod, J. (2007). A pluralistic framework for counselling and psychotherapy: Implications for research. *Counselling and Psychotherapy Research 7*(3), 135–143. Accessed on 3/11/2021 at https://doi.org/10.1080/14733140701566282

Doran, G.T. (1981). There's a SMART way to write management's goals and objectives. *Management Review 70*(11), 35–36.

Geretsegger, M., Holck, U., Carpente, J.A., Elefant, C., Kim, J. & Gold, C. (2015). Common characteristics of improvisational approaches in music therapy for children with autism spectrum disorder: Developing treatment guidelines. *Journal of Music Therapy 52*(2), 258–281. Accessed on 3/11/2021 at https://doi.org/10.1093/jmt/thv005

Gfeller, K.E. & Davis, W.B. (2008). The Music Therapy Treatment Process. In W.B. Davis, K.E. Gfeller & M.H. Thaut (eds) *An Introduction to Music Therapy Theory and Practice*. Silver Spring, MD: American Music Therapy Association.

Hanser, S.B. (2018). *The New Music Therapist's Handbook* (3rd edn). Boston, MA: Berklee Press.

Hardy, M.W. & LaGasse, A.B. (2018). Music Therapy for Persons with Autism Spectrum Disorder. In A. Knight, A.B. LaGasse, & A. Clair (eds) *Music Therapy: An Introduction to the Profession*. Silver Springs, MD: American Music Therapy Association.

Havsteen-Franklin, D., Jovanovic, N., Reed, N., Charles, M. & Lucas, C. (2017). Developing a shared language within arts psychotherapies: A personal construct psychology approach to understanding clinical change. *The Arts in Psychotherapy 55*, 103–110. Accessed on 3/11/2021 at https://doi.org/10.1016/j.aip.2017.05.002

Jacob, J., Edbrooke-Childs, J., Holley, S., Law, D. & Wolpert, M. (2016). Horses for courses? A qualitative exploration of goals formulated in mental health settings by young people, parents, and clinicians. *Clinical Child Psychology and Psychiatry 21*(2), 208–223. Accessed on 3/11/2021 at https://doi.org/10.1177/1359104515577487

Jacobsen, S.L. & Thompson, G. (2016). Working with Families: Emerging Characteristics. In S.L. Jacobson & G. Thompson (eds), *Music Therapy with Families: Therapeutic Approaches and Theoretical Perspectives*. London: Jessica Kingsley Publishers.

Jung, L.A. (2007). Writing SMART objectives and strategies that fit the ROUTINE. *Teaching Exceptional Children 39*(4), 54–58. Accessed on 3/11/2021 at https://doi.org/10.1177/004005990703900406

Kanowski, S. (2018). What Jack Reacher did next [Audio podcast episode]. In *Conversations with Richard Fidler, Sarah Kanowski*. ABC, 30 November. Accessed on 3/11/2021 at www.abc.net.au/radio/programs/conversations/lee-child-2018/10551066

Kaplan, R.S. & Steele, A.L. (2005). An analysis of music therapy program goals and outcomes for clients with diagnoses on the autism spectrum. *Journal of Music Therapy 42*(1), 2–19.

Lee, J., Teggelove, K., Tamplin, J., Thompson, G., Murphy, M. & McFerran, K.S. (2018). Whose choice? Exploring multiple perspectives on music therapy access under the National Disability Insurance Scheme. *Australian Journal of Music Therapy 29*, 91–115.

Loewy, J. (2000). Music psychotherapy assessment. *Music Therapy Perspectives 18*(1), 47–58. Accessed on 5/4/2022 at https://doi.org/10.1093/mtp/18.1.47

Martikainen, P., Bartley, M. & Lahelma, E. (2002). Psychosocial determinants of health in social epidemiology. *International Journal of Epidemiology 31*, 1091–1093.

McFerran, K.S. & Rickson, D. (2014). Community music therapy in schools: Realigning with the needs of contemporary students, staff and systems. *International Journal of Community Music 7*(1), 75–92. Accessed on 3/11/2021 at https://doi.org/10.1386/ijcm.7.1.75_1

McGuire, A.B., Oles, S.K., White, D.A. & Salyers, M.P. (2016). Perceptions of treatment plan goals of people in psychiatric rehabilitation. *Journal of Behavioral Health Services & Research 43*(3), 494–503. Accessed on 3/11/2021 at https://doi.org/10.1007/s11414-015-9463-x

Molyneux, C., Koo, N.-H., Piggot-Irvine, E., Talmage, A., Travaglia, R. & Willis, M. (2012). Doing it together: Collaborative research on goal-setting and review in a music therapy centre. *New Zealand Journal of Music Therapy 10*, 6–38.

NDIS (2019). How the planning process works. Accessed on 3/11/2021 at www.ndis.gov.au/participants/how-planning-process-works

NDIS (2021). Independent Assessment Framework. Accessed on 12/11/2021 at https://ndis.gov.au/media/2672/download

Norris, M. & Kilbride, C. (2014). From dictatorship to a reluctant democracy: Stroke therapists talking about self-management. *Disability and Rehabilitation 36*(1), 32–38. Accessed on 31/01/2022 at https://doi.org/10.3109/09638288.2013.776645

Odhammar, F. & Carlberg, G. (2015). Parents' and psychotherapists' goals prior to psychodynamic child psychotherapy. *European Journal of Psychotherapy & Counselling 17*(3), 277–295. Accessed on 3/11/2021 at https://doi.org/10.1080/13642537.2015.1059865

Pickard, B., Thompson, G., Metell, M., Roginsky, E. & Elefant, C. (2020). 'It's not what's done, but *why* it's done': Music therapists' understanding of normalisation, maximisation and the neurodiversity movement. *Voices: A World Forum for Music Therapy 20*(3). Accessed on 3/11/2021 at https://voices.no/index.php/voices/article/view/3110/3067?fbclid=IwARonUsnMjbTn46QvHBikAaxEoUdiU-EHkoVq6hhIMmd-i_JpQMzSeol_Qbdo

Polen, D.W., Shultis, C.L. & Wheeler, B. (2017). *Clinical Training Guide for the Student Music Therapist* (2nd edn). New Braunfels, TX: Barcelona Publishers.

Poulsen, A., Ziviani, J.M. & Cuskelly, M. (2015). The Science of Goal Setting. In A. Poulsen, J.M. Ziviani & M. Cuskelly (eds), *Goal Setting and Motivation in Therapy: Engaging Children and Parents*. London: Jessica Kingsley Publishers.

Rolvsjord, R. (2010). *Resource-Oriented Music Therapy in Mental Health Care*. New Braunfels, TX: Barcelona Publishers.

Rolvsjord, R. (2015). What clients do to make music therapy work: A qualitative multiple case study in adult mental health care. *Nordic Journal of Music Therapy 24*(4), 296–321. Accessed on 3/11/2021 at https://doi.org/10.1080/08098131.2014.964753

Sena Moore, K. & LaGasse, A.B. (2018). Parallels and divergence between neuroscience and humanism: Considerations for the music therapist. *Music Therapy Perspectives 36*(2), 144–151. Accessed on 3/11/2021 at https://doi.org/10.1093/mtp/miyo11

Stige, B. (2002). *Culture-Centered Music Therapy*. New Braunfels, TX: Barcelona Publishers.

Stige, B. & Aarø, L. (2011). *Invitation to Community Music Therapy*. New York, NY, and London: Routledge.

Thompson, G. (2016). Families with Preschool-Aged Children with Autism Spectrum Disorder. In S.L. Jacobson & G. Thompson (eds) *Music Therapy with Families: Therapeutic Approaches and Theoretical Perspectives*. London: Jessica Kingsley Publishers.

Tryon, G.S. & Winograd, G. (2011). Goal consensus and collaboration. *Psychotherapy* 48(1), 50–57. Accessed on 3/11/2021 at https://doi.org/10.1037/a0022061

Vaillancourt, G. (2012). Music therapy: A community approach to social justice. *The Arts in Psychotherapy 39*(3), 173–178. Accessed on 3/11/2021 at https://doi.org/10.1016/j.aip.2011.12.011

Wallen, M. & Stewart, K. (2015). The GAS Approach: Scaling Tailored Goals. In J.M. Ziviani, A. Poulsen & M. Cuskelly (eds), *Goal Setting and Motivation in Therapy: Engaging Children and Parents*. London: Jessica Kingsley Publishers.

PART 2

A THEORY OF GOAL PROCESSES

CHAPTER 3

Introduction to the client-in-context theory

TOWARDS A THEORY OF GOAL PROCESSES

Supervisors and educators can be tempted to offer protocols and practice guidelines as a way to clarify complex professional concepts to their supervisees and learners. However, such protocols and practices are often brittle and rigid. Theory, on the other hand, provides a system of ideas or general principles that are intended to be flexible and adaptive to a multitude of situations. A theory can therefore be applied and interpreted with suitable consideration for the context. Theories can be developed in various ways. Within the research context, the method of grounded theory was developed by Barney Glaser and Anselm Strauss who believed that theory could be revealed within data collected through social (qualitative) research. Theory derived in this way was considered to be more directly relevant to the actual real-life topic under consideration, and therefore would be 'grounded' and 'substantive' (Glaser & Strauss, 1967).

Within the music therapy literature, many authors have described and provided examples of goal-writing approaches based on their wealth of practice experience, but there is limited research available. Abbott's (2020) survey research from the USA is an exception, with this study investigating the real-world goal and objective writing practices reported by music therapists. The data is categorized into key features and components of goals and objectives, as described by the participants. Therefore, this research can inform better goal-writing practices in music therapy. However, as noted in Chapter 2, Abbott (2020) acknowledges that writing skills are only one aspect to consider, and that music therapists also need to adapt their approach to the philosophies and conventions in each setting. This sentiment is supported by statements made by several participants in my own grounded theory research project who wanted to encourage music therapy trainees and new graduates to develop flexibility, respon-siveness, and reflexivity around their goal processes. Having too much focus on writing skills or guidelines without the companion of reflexivity was considered less than ideal by some participants, such as Domenico from Italy:

> If a student comes to supervision and asks, 'What should I do?', and if a teacher tells them, 'You should try this or you should try that', that has eliminated the awareness process of reflection for the student. So, teachers have to help students to continue to navigate, within a bit of frustration of not knowing, but still going further, which is a bit of a paradox. But I think that [approach] is safer than saying, 'Do this or that', or 'Try this or that', because that eliminates reflection... [What we need] in the long run is a therapist who is more capable of adapting to the specific needs and the specific goals of their clients.

Domenico from Italy

The limited research on this topic is surprising. While the practice wisdom of authors of individual texts and articles is valuable, what is missing is exactly what was advocated for by Glaser and Strauss (1967) in their seminal work: theory that is grounded in real-life data through systematic coding and categorization. While our profes-sional standards of practice can outline a framework of procedures around goals, these documents cannot support practitioners to understand how to identify the goal or write it. Only theory can articulate foundational principles and posit relationships between constructs to help individuals to *understand and articulate why we do what we do in the way we do it*. The research underpinning this book therefore centres around gaining a better understanding of goal processes rather than goal writing, and advocates for an alternative to protocols that imply a one-size-fits-all approach.

THE RESEARCH CONTEXT

To address the gap in the literature, I set out to collect data that would represent a range of perspectives and standpoints (Thompson, 2020). Doing so would enable the grounded theory to have the potential for relevance beyond a particular orientation to practice, cultural context, or area of specialty. I therefore invited music therapists who had at least five years of experience in either supervising or teaching music therapy students (or both) to participate in an in-depth interview. The final sample included 45 music therapists (female n = 31, 69 %) ranging in age from 33 to 67 years old and having between 5 and 42 years of professional experience. Of these, 25 were teachers in tertiary-level training courses, five were clinical supervisors, and 15 were both educators and supervisors. Participants were living and working in eight different countries, including the United States (n=13 from four cities), England (n=5), Scotland (n=4), Norway (n=8), Denmark (n=6), Italy (n=5), Australia (n=2), South Korea (n=1), and Israel (n=1).

In terms of clinical experience, 31 participants worked predominantly with children and youth (54%), while 26 worked predominantly with adults (46%). Based on participants' descriptions of their practice, 19 broad clinical categories could be determined that represent a wide variety of practice specializations. The most prominent practice areas of specialty were mental health, disability, and autism (see Table 3.1).

Table 3.1: Practice areas of the research participants

Practice area	Number of participants
Disability (physical and/or intellectual)	17
Mental health/psychiatry	17
Autism/neurodevelopmental	6
Family	5
Dementia	4
Addiction	3
Neonatal Intensive Care Unit (NICU)	3
Paediatrics	3
Schools	3
Oncology	2
Medical	2
Brain injury	2
Trauma	2
Guided Imagery in Music (GIM)	2
Palliative care	1
Parkinson's disease	1
Older adults	1
Residential care	1
Adoption	1

I asked each participant to first describe the theoretical influences in their work. The majority described multiple frameworks, with an average of 3.48 per person. Humanistic and psychodynamic influences were the most common; however, there were 31 theoretical frameworks described by the participants (see Table 3.2).

Table 3.2: Theories informing the practice of the research participants

Theory	Number of participants
Humanistic	27
Psychodynamic	24

Developmental/relational (Stern, Developmental Individual-difference Relationship-based model (DIR Floortime®), play theory)	18
Music centred	8
Systems thinking/ecological	7
Existential	6
Psychoanalytic	5
Community music therapy	5
Resource oriented	5
Behavioural (including Dialectical behavioural therapy (DBT) or Cognitive behavioural therapy (CBT))	5
Improvisational (Wigram/Bruscia)	4
Nordoff Robbins	4
Neurological (broad or Neurological Music Therapy (NMT))	3
Attachment	3
GIM	3
Phenomenology	2
Alvin model	2
Mentalization	2
Hermeneutics	1
Priestly model	1
Integrative	1
Ethnomusicology: Trance and consciousness	1
Neuroaffective (trauma theory)	1
Field of Play (Kenny)	1
Biopsychosocial	1
Musicology	1
Sociology	1
Positive psychology	1
Joanne Loewy model	1
Critical theory	1
Integral thinking (Wilbur)	1

Next, I invited participants to describe: (1) their approach to goals/ aims within their own music therapy practice, (2) what they consider to be the main factors that influence their approach to goals/ aims, and (3) what they consider to be important when supporting students to understand goals/aims in music therapy. The responses to these prompt questions were then analyzed to build the resultant grounded theory.

THE 'CLIENT-IN-CONTEXT' THEORY FOR IDENTIFYING A THERAPEUTIC FOCUS IN MUSIC THERAPY

The music therapy educators and senior clinicians interviewed expressed in various ways that the process of *identifying a therapeutic focus* was a core part of their professional role. Different terms were used to describe the product of this process, such as goals, aims, direction, or focus. For this reason, I avoided labelling the central category as 'identifying a *goal*'. Instead, the label 'identifying a therapeutic focus' intends to soften and broaden the possibilities for the form a goal might take in different situations. Readers can substitute the phrase 'identifying a therapeutic focus' with the term that best applies in their context, such as goal, objective, short-term aim, long-term aim, aim, direction, focus, or purpose.

The interviewees did acknowledge the importance of developing skills in the technical aspects of goal writing, such as alignment with the client's needs, checking for relevance and feasibility, and complementing the intentions of the broader team. However, these practical concerns were overshadowed by their rich descriptions of the conditions that influence *how* the therapist goes about identifying a therapeutic focus, and the possible resulting consequences.

The central category, 'identifying a therapeutic focus', was therefore conceived because every participant, no matter the term they used, stated in some way that therapy must always have a purpose.

58

Clara, a music therapist from Denmark, describes the importance of having a direction to the quality of her work as a therapist:

> [Having a direction] gives you the confidence to actually let go and be present. Because when you're confident and you know that 'I'm on to something important here', you can also let go. If you're very uncertain of what you're doing, you're not...going to be able to be present in the moment... So goal setting is essential. Both theoretically and practically; if you don't know where you're going, or even why you're going anywhere, there is a huge risk. It's going to be unethical, or it's going to be meaningless, or...you have no means of monitoring anything if you don't have a standpoint before you take off.

Clara from Denmark

Other participants went so far as to say it would be impossible for a therapist to facilitate a therapy session and not have some idea of what they hope to offer, or that it would 'end up being lazy sloppy work' if a therapist doesn't try to negotiate goals of some kind with the person they are working with (Jarle from Norway). It strikes me that the central category 'identifying a therapeutic focus' further reinforces the notion that goal processes themselves are at the heart of overall therapy processes. Antonio from Italy explains the importance of goals processes in this way:

> Producing goals, [and] writing goals, does not produce only goals. It produces thinking. It produces something inside us... [It's] good to think about goals not as a solution but as a way to produce thinking.

Antonio from Italy

However, as with all things, balance is the key. While all the participants considered that having a focus was essential in therapy work, many also identified risks if the goal became rigidly followed or valued for its own sake. Frederik from Denmark reflected that if a therapist was only 'committed to fulfilling a goal instead of being aware of the needs of [the people they work with]', then they are equally not fulfilling their role. Complexity abounds within this process, and the resultant grounded theory provides a notional compass to help guide therapists in their own reflexivity, or with the support of a supervisor.

Invitation to reflexivity: Antonio from Italy said, 'Producing goals, [and] writing goals, does not produce only goals. It produces thinking.' What do you consider when trying to articulate the goal or direction of music therapy sessions? What aspects of your practice do you think about when planning goals?

Moving on from the central category, the music therapists identified three distinct aspects that influence the process for identifying a therapeutic focus: namely, (1) the music therapist's attributes, (2) the client's attributes, and (3) the features of the context.[1] The therapist's professional responsibility was therefore viewed as working to meet the needs of the client-in-context (Thompson, 2020). The full theory is represented as a diagram in Figure 3.1.

---

[1]   The term 'context' refers to the institution, employer, referrer, funder, family member or individual who either pays the therapist or has governance/responsibility for the health of the client. A therapist running their own private practice would also be considered relevant to this notion of context.

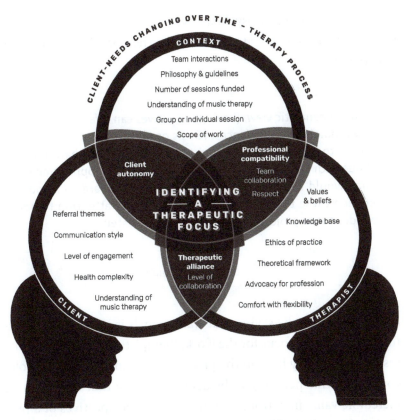

Figure 3.1: The client-in-context theory, reproduced from Thompson (2020)

The qualities that these three aspects bring to the process, and how they *interact* with each other, impacts both the way the therapeutic focus is identified and the essence of the focus itself. I have therefore attempted to visually represent the overall relational power dynamics through the Venn diagram. For example, the client and therapist are facing each other, and the context floats above them both. Each player is interconnected, and the qualities and attributes of all three influence the therapeutic focus. Perhaps this representation might suggest that power is harmoniously and equally distributed between each player. However, several participants in the research project described various forms of power tensions dynamically shifting between each of these players. Antonio, a music therapist from Italy, reflected deeply on the internal power processes for himself as a therapist. Informed by psychoanalytic theories, he identified that there could be defences at play when the therapeutic focus is being negotiated:

> In a psychoanalytic view, [having] objectives can refer to defences and even...obsessive defences. [Goals or objectives] control what is going to happen... So [therapists] are [like] an acrobat; to not collude with the system's defences, [and] not to be [oppositional], which would be another type of defence. So we are an acrobat between these two things, and we have to pay attention to not collude, not to project, our defences on the system.

Antonio from Italy

Antonio seems to be saying that stating goals is inherently powerful. By declaring a focus for the work, therapists must recognize the responsibility they have in the process. Antonio's colleague, Paolo, contrasted this perspective by acknowledging that there can be incredible value in considering the multiple perspectives of a professional team. Through metaphor, Paolo explains the importance of multiple perspectives:

> Within multidisciplinary work, one approach is that, when various professions meet together, that might be a level where the goal [can benefit from the] various ingredients. For example, when a poet goes to a forest, he sees the forest and the trees with the eyes of a poet. If a carpenter goes to the forest, he sees a chair, a table. So this difference of perspective, and integrating [each of] them and respecting them, can create an all-around vision of the person in that case.

Paolo from Italy

Paolo's reflection on the contributions and interactions of each team member highlights that each player needs to be considered both individually and collectively.

Within each aspect of this theory, there are various qualities to discuss, as well as considering how each aspect might interact together. Chapters 4 to 7 explore the three main players in this theory, namely the therapist, the client, and the context, followed by considering the interactions between them. Quotations from participants and reflexive tasks will help to bring this theory to life. Later in Part 3, I will provide examples of the application of this theory through composite case examples drawn from the stories shared by the participants, and also suggest some practical guidelines for the technical aspects of goal writing.

REFERENCES

Abbott, E.A. (2020). Music therapists' goal and objective writing practices. *Music Therapy Perspectives 38*(2), 178–186. Accessed on 3/11/2021 at https://doi.org/10.1093/mtp/miz018

Glaser, B.G. & Strauss, A. (1967). *The Discovery of Grounded Theory: Strategies for Qualitative Research*. Piscataway, NJ: Aldine.

Thompson, G.A. (2020). A grounded theory of music therapists' approach to goal processes within their clinical practice. *The Arts in Psychotherapy 70*. Accessed on 3/11/2021 at https://doi.org/10.1016/j.aip.2020.101680

CHAPTER 4

The music therapist's attributes

Having presented a summary of the client-in-context theory in Chapter 3, I will now describe in depth the attributes that the music therapist brings to the process of identifying a therapeutic focus. These attributes include the therapist's *personal values and beliefs*, which in turn are strongly related to the *theoretical frameworks* with which they choose to align. The therapist's practice *knowledge*, developed through their training and years of experience with a particular population, helps them to understand the types of focus areas that are likely to be relevant and meaningful. Alongside this knowledge, the therapist's *ethics of practice* is a strong factor in their work, particularly when working with people who have complex health needs that leave them seriously vulnerable to an imbalance of power. Since people's needs may change moment to moment or over a longer period of time, the therapist's *comfort with flexibility* can also influence the process of identifying a focus for the work. The music therapist may also consider the degree to which they wish to *advocate* for greater understanding of their scope of practice through clearly articulating a certain type of therapeutic focus to the client and the service context (see Figure 4.1). Each of these categories is further elaborated below.

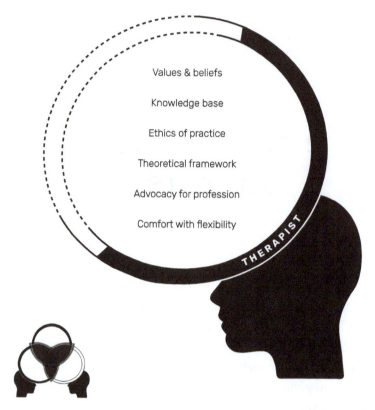

Values & beliefs

Knowledge base

Ethics of practice

Theoretical framework

Advocacy for profession

Comfort with flexibility

THERAPIST

Figure 4.1: The therapist's attributes

PERSONAL VALUES AND BELIEFS

The therapist's personal values and beliefs permeate the way they approach goal processes, either consciously or unconsciously. In the interviews with experienced music therapists, the majority described the 'overarching goals' or 'meta-goals' that inform their approach to practice. These overarching goals could also be seen as statements of their personal values and beliefs about music therapy, music engagement, therapeutic relationships, and the meaning of their work. Consider the following statements:

My goal is to create or to co-create an environment or a context of care, of humanity, of dignity.

Theo from the USA

You just search for a place where your client is another human being and where you forget the diagnosis. So that's also a kind of goal in a way, a humanistic way of being in the world with other people.

Luna from Denmark

When I'm going into the session, all that I'm thinking about really is 'How am I going to engage [the child]?'

Paul from the USA

I've often thought about just 'being with' [the person]. So that could be a focus for someone with dementia. It might be, well, you're with them in that moment.

Olivia from England

I've always had the strong belief that in music therapy there's a lot that grows out of the relationship. The musical and personal relationship that happens in musicking... That's where I'm really interested in seeing what happens. But I don't suppose I write that as a goal, or anything related to that.

Amy from Australia

> [I have] a very general basis of providing a space where the person or the group express or communicate and be listened to. Those I would say are my general underlining goals.

Domenico from Italy

These interview snapshots reveal the powerful ways that the therapists' values and beliefs underpin their work. Acknowledging the values that drive practice can help therapists to understand why they might be drawn to certain types of work or why they are struggling to work in settings that clash with their own beliefs. Greater awareness of our values and beliefs might also create new possibilities for professional conversations with our colleagues and managers.

THEORETICAL FRAMEWORKS

Therapists' values and beliefs might originate from many different sources, such as their lived experience, culture, spirituality, and family to name a few. As we study to achieve our qualifications, the training course will also introduce us to various theoretical frameworks. Later, continuing professional development may introduce further theories that become incorporated into our practice. In order to highlight the way these frameworks interact with each therapist's values and beliefs and flow through to practice, I have selected three perspectives from the interview participants. First, Agnes, an experienced clinician and educator in music therapy, explains the influence that a training course might have on our subsequent practice:

I have been trained in the tradition of understanding transfer issues in therapeutic relationships. I have been trained in the tradition... that your unconscious is important, and some important underlying forces also have an influence. So, of course, this is part of [my foundation]. And it doesn't mean that I think people shouldn't do functional or neurological music therapy or other approaches if this is relevant. But [I believe these therapists] still must have a consciousness about positions and perceptions as something basic and grounding. And I think in some ways it influences the way they understand themselves in their role as a therapist.

Agnes from Denmark

As described in Chapter 3, the participants in this research were overall informed by 31 theoretical frameworks, with 40 out of 45 people working from multiple perspectives. In a similar way to their values and beliefs, these philosophies also underpinned the way they approached identifying the therapeutic focus of their work. As Agnes states above, these philosophies are 'basic and grounding' to practice.

The next two quotes highlight very different 'basic and grounding' philosophies that inform each person's approach to writing goals: neurological understandings of music therapy; followed by a community music therapy orientation.

Well, [goals are] entirely informed by the essentials, which are: what's the diagnosis/prognosis? What are the observations by the multidisciplinary members...and family if they're involved? And then, what's the output? What happens when I then present some musical task or interaction or something with that person?

George from England; informed by neurological theories

In my own doctoral thesis about Community Music Therapy... participants wanted to play with the local [musicians], which was absolutely beyond my concept of music therapy. But...they challenged my thinking by describing what they wanted to do. So that's always been important for me to try and kind of understand where that person comes from and where that person wants to go... I guess my way of work has very much been goal negotiation. Which would come from, I think, with humanistic influence. That the goals wouldn't be...expert defined, or they would not be functional necessarily. [The goals would] be about the person's own hopes and desires for participation in the world. So negotiation between the two of us... Helping them to find this direction is very much the way I've been working as a music therapist.

Jarle from Norway

Agnes, George, and Jarle are thinking about and approaching goal processes in very different ways based on the combination of their philosophical understanding of music therapy and their own values and beliefs. Each of these therapists is well respected in their field and has an advanced concept of their professional work. Yet the differences between them are likely to lead to vastly different therapeutic foci. Nonetheless, the people they work with are also likely to experience meaningful personal outcomes. This complexity is essential to understand so that therapists can work reflexively and continue to critically evaluate their approach to practice.

Invitation to reflexivity: Map out your values and beliefs, and your theoretical influences. In what ways do these beliefs and philosophies drive your practice (or not)?

KNOWLEDGE

Alongside personal values and beliefs, and the fundamental under-standings of our philosophical approach, therapists also need to build their professional knowledge base. The therapist must balance their understanding of general information about, for example, certain health conditions, lifespan stages, life-changing events, and cultural identities with their ability to be curious about the uniqueness of each individual. The therapist's general knowledge may help them to 'zone in' on certain domains or skills for goal writing. Freja from Denmark specializes in working with autistic children and explains that her first step is to consider 'What do I know about autism? What needs do these children have according to the general autism literature?' George from England specializes in working with people following brain injuries and considers the essential knowledge informing his goals are 'the diagnosis/prognosis...[and] the observations by the multidisciplinary members'.

The research participants also acknowledged that assessment processes are central to the therapist's knowledge about the person they are working with. This is one instance where it is difficult to talk in isolation about only one element of practice such as goals. Knowledge gained through observation, getting to know the person, and listening to the person/team/family are all relevant here. Ruby, from the USA, explained what she considers important when inte-grating knowledge from various sources, and how she guides her music therapy students:

> I want [students] to be able to describe what they're seeing and not just make an assumption or put that assessment on someone... To really be reflexive about what it is that they're doing and seeing, and not just jump to conclusions about the way that they see a client behaving in a group.

Ruby from the USA

ETHICS OF PRACTICE

Music and creative arts therapists work with a variety of people, many of whom have idiosyncratic forms of communication that take time to understand and appreciate. In some instances, the therapist might never feel completely confident that they understand what the person wants from therapy. Even when working with people who can communicate with words, text, or other symbolic forms, there can be factors that limit their ability to identify or share their wishes and needs. This serious ethical responsibility within goal processes was acknowledged in some way by nearly every participant contributing to this theory. Franco from Italy powerfully explains:

> Goals are a crucial point and an ethical point, because the goal is always based on a change and transformation inside the person; the music therapist must have an ethical responsibility about that part... Because change in another person is really a huge responsibility. Especially because we work with the child or people who are not able to decide, who are not free to decide... So we really have a double responsibility.

Franco from Italy

Ethical complexities abound and need specific consideration depending on the practice context. For example, family-centred orientations require the music therapist to first consider who is the 'client' and, therefore, the focus of the goal. For example, often the family member with a particular diagnosis is the one referred to music therapy. However, the family dynamics will also influence the nature of the work. A music therapist who works with families might acknowledge that they have an overarching goal to 'strengthen family relationships', yet the specific goals they write may only focus on the family member with the diagnosis. This creates a potential ethical dilemma around transparency of practice. Lily, an experienced family-centred music therapist from England, acknowledges the ethical complexity as follows:

If it's the child that's been referred, then it's the child who we're specifying the aims for. Occasionally, parents will [say to me], 'You know, I really would like some ideas of how to work with my child.' But mostly, [parents] come [and say], 'My child. What are we going to do [for my child]?' So, you have to get to the point gradually where you're working in partnership with the parents. Because some parents would run a mile if you said, 'Actually, this work is mainly for you rather than your child.' Some wouldn't, but some would. You know, they come with the idea that this is really to help their child. And as I see it, I've got to help the family. I've got to help the parent interact with the child. I've got to, yes, make a connection with the child, but then help the parent to enhance that connection... But it is often not so clearly out there. Because actually, some of the families wouldn't like to see it like that.

Lily from England

A further ethical consideration for music therapists centres around continuing to weigh up the relevance of the goals that have been identified for the client, particularly if they have been written by the broader team. As discussed from the outset, goals are powerful statements that also form the basis for evaluating outcomes in many organizations and contexts. Therapists can find themselves in the situation where they don't agree with the focus of work identified by the broader team and will need to consider the ethics of their practice. Rebecca from Norway reflects on her work as follows:

I was always trying to figure out, how do we make this more meaningful? Because to me it gets very close to feeling like you're doing something to someone, and you're creating these goals, especially [for an autistic child], you're doing something that you think is good for them. And you do it to them because perhaps they're not able to express what they want or how they want to be seen or so forth.

Rebecca from Norway

It seems important, then, for music therapists to deeply consider not only the content of the goal but also how specific it needs to be, and how flexibly the therapist will facilitate the therapy sessions. There is a sense here of balancing potential risks: the risk of having too little direction in therapy, with the risk of having too much direction with no flexibility. Jarle from Norway notes that the policy systems therapists work within can also give mixed messages in regard to the need for clearly articulated goals and a desire for people's choice and control. Jarle reflected that these systems can sometimes create confusion for therapists, particularly for those who are in training or in the early stage of their careers:

In our health care system now, there's more [emphasis] on the patient's right to choose. So I think there's also some kind of ambiva- lence in the society. At one side, there's a drive for...defining goals functionally and [clear] procedures. And at the other side it's the democratic, collaborative, negotiated [approach]. So, two things are going on at the same time. So students might be confused by having at least two quite different influences from society actually... And these [government policy] guidelines, they are very often written with a kind of mixed discourse. You know, there's kind of this evidence-based medicine logic, that we [only] recommend those things which have evidence. But at the same time, it's recovery [model] thinking: that the person should define the goals for his or her own life. And those two rhetorics, they don't go perfectly together.

Jarle from Norway

Invitation to reflexivity: What do you consider to be the main ethical challenge in your practice?

COMFORT WITH FLEXIBILITY

It seems that one of the ways therapists can navigate these complex ethical considerations is to determine how much flexibility they will include in their approach as a kind of safeguard to the risks they identify with being too rigid. The therapist must determine how long to focus on a particular goal, how the goals will be refined or updated and how will they be negotiated with the people they work with and the team. Frederik from Denmark explains his flexible approach by making a distinction between 'formal' goals that may have been identified after an assessment process, and 'here-and-now' goals that emerge from a particular moment in the session and therefore require immediate attention:

> [The music therapist must be] able to navigate in the here-and-now of what is the need of the client. And I think that is a very fundamental experience and element in our teaching [and training]. That [all at the same time, the therapist] tries to have an idea of where you're going, and can also totally let go of this and be able to navigate what's in front of you.

Frederik from Denmark

Even for therapists who have a strong belief in following predetermined goals, working with the person's here-and-now needs cannot be ignored. Carol from the USA explains:

> One of the things that we teach our students is the iso principle, so that you start wherever your client is. And your predetermined goal does not necessarily change. How you get there is what changes based upon where the client is.

Carol from the USA

However, the degree of flexibility a therapist can adopt also intersects with ethical considerations, since sometimes working with the person's here-and-now needs may open up completely different opportunities. A therapist who feels obligated to their predetermined goal may miss an important possibility in the work. Jarle powerfully explains:

> In my experience...when working with intellectually disabled people, playing with a [local] band would absolutely not be something I would articulate. And it turned out to be so, so important for these people. And also within a mental health context, the person will end up doing things in the community, for instance, in supplement with the therapy in the clinic. [These community experiences] would become a very, very important part of the process, like becoming a volunteer or becoming a member of a choir or something. And I wouldn't be able to define that from the start, and the person wouldn't be able to define that from the start, but it would evolve in the process.

Jarle from Norway

PROFESSIONAL ADVOCACY

For some music therapists, the way goals are written has the potential to be a form of professional advocacy. When we articulate what is happening in music therapy through goals and objectives, these documents can shape the way other professionals and community members perceive our work. Franco from Italy explains:

> I think also that goals and assessment are very important for the recognition of the profession because we are trying to have a professional level in which the music therapists are able to project, to realize, and to assess clinical music therapy work collaborating with teamwork and under the supervision of a medical doctor. Goals and assessment mean that you are able to evaluate and give value to your clinical work.

Franco from Italy

Some music therapists may want to ensure that the goals articulate the distinct benefits of music therapy or the opportunities that music experiences offer to the therapeutic process. Others, on the other hand, see the benefit in using more generic language in their goals to highlight that music therapy is a legitimate way to address general domains of health. Further, the potential for a goal or objective to be evaluated quantitatively might be a powerful form of advocacy to demonstrate change and growth. Mary from Scotland explains how her work with a young man with complex needs could be documented and evaluated in multiple ways:

I'm working with a young man at the moment who has a severe learning disability, a very sort of vibrant young man. And it feels very...it's hard to say...not behavioural, but there is a focus on [fostering] one-to-one interaction for more than three or four minutes. [This goal] feels much more sort of prescriptive almost. But actually it's thinking about, well, the wider impact of that. How is that going to be beneficial? But within that, [there is] the creativity and also the freedom to play [music] and to be very much client-led going on... So...it's prescriptive in so far as [the goal is] to increase this person's ability to turn-take. But within that, also thinking about [this young man's] own kind of creative potential. So it's not just ticking a box that, well, you know, we've been improving aspects of his social interaction, but also, you know this...the very person-centred element of it. That actually, [I'm considering] what's he getting from [music therapy] emotionally, and being in a relationship with someone through music.

Mary from Scotland

The attributes of the music therapist interact and combine in various ways to inform goal processes. Each element might be more or less prominent in our practice, and the impact of these elements is likely to change over time. Reflecting on our own attributes can be a powerful way to understand aspects of goal writing that can feel difficult and easy for us. New insights can sometimes quickly emerge,

CHAPTER 5

The client's attributes

MUTUALITY AND AGENCY

In the diagram representing the client-in-context theory (Figure 3.1), therapist and client are facing each other. This is fundamental because each of these players exists in relation to the other. They share a metaphorical 'mutual gaze' or 'being with' the other. For the therapist, 'being with' the person carries with it an ethical responsibility, as explored in Chapter 4. For the person themselves, various factors may lead to more or less agency in the therapy process, as well as factors that influence the sense of shared experience with the therapist. By interviewing therapists, we can only have a particular perspective of the ways that clients' attributes influence goal processes. Nonetheless, the interviewees identified several aspects related to the people they work with that were considered key to their understanding of goal processes.

Starting with the *referral themes*, some participants believed that the reasons a person comes to therapy provide enough focus in the initial stages of the work, before a more refined aim/goal/objective is identified. Moving on from the referral, the client's *health complexity* and *communication style* are significant factors impacting the way the therapeutic focus is determined. The participants acknowledged that the people they work with may or may not be able to communicate in conventional ways, and so the therapist requires time to come to an understanding of the person's needs through assessment processes, developing a relationship with the person, and collaboration with team members. The people they work with will have varying degrees of *understanding music therapy*, which also impacts the focus of the work. For example, some people may prefer to focus on the tangible aspects of musical experience, such as writing a song or playing an instrument, while others may have limited awareness of their reason for being referred to music therapy and rely on the therapist to provide a direction. The person's *level of engagement* in various aspects of their therapy process, from the reason why they are participating in music therapy to their interest in music making, will also impact the process of identifying a therapeutic focus (see Figure 5.1). Each of these categories is further elaborated below.

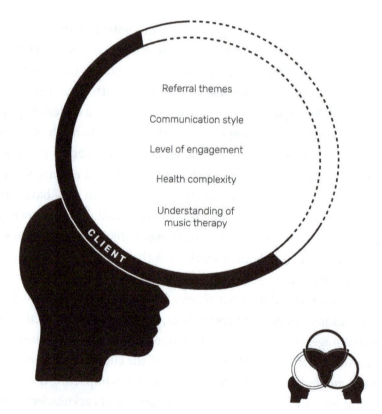

Referral themes

Communication style

Level of engagement

Health complexity

Understanding of
music therapy

CLIENT

Figure 5.1: The client's attributes

REFERRAL THEMES

Identifying a therapeutic focus often begins with the reasons for referral. The wide variety of contexts within which music therapists work results in different forms of referral. In some contexts, a person will refer themselves to music therapy. In others, a family member or professional will refer the person to music therapy. As a starting point, the referral can provide the music therapist with preliminary information about the person's health, sense of agency, and level of understanding about music therapy in general. The way a person responds to music experiences or answers open questions such as 'What brings you to music therapy?' or 'What would you like to do in music therapy?' become the starting point for the therapeutic relationship.

HEALTH COMPLEXITY

I imagine (or hope) that most therapists will want to foster agency in the people they work with, particularly when determining the focus of the person's therapy. There are times, however, when clients may feel stressed by the invitation to collaborate or overwhelmed by the possibilities within music therapy. Similarly, family members (parents, spouses, adult children) may have their own pressures and feel overwhelmed by the responsibility of collaborating with the therapist.

Therapists may need to be mindful that, in the initial stages, the people they work with might feel safer if the therapist takes the lead in presenting some opportunities or music experiences to commence the work together. For example, when working with people who have neurological impairments, their ability to identify a need or focus will influence the level of collaboration with the therapist. Liv from Norway reflected on her work with people with dementia and the potential distress it might cause to have a collaborative or direct conversation about goals:

> [For people with dementia] it is possible to talk and to agree [on the focus] in that way. But sometimes it's not...it's in a way not right to do that. It can be very difficult, because they might not understand, and they might not have insight into their own condition.

Liv from Norway

As Liv suggests, the person's level of insight into their condition is a particularly challenging aspect for music therapists to consider when they wish to collaborate in goal processes. Agnes from Denmark deeply considered these challenges when describing her work with a person with mental illness:

> The client at that time did not express any kind of goal, because she was not very aware that she had any kind of symptoms, and she didn't want to be aware. She could not articulate what she wanted to do in the therapy. I discussed this very often with [my colleagues] because some professionals always have the ideal that we need to meet the needs of the clients. And, of course, we do. But very often I also told [my colleagues], 'But who knows about the needs of the client?' In this example here, with this lady with [mental illness], if you asked her about her needs, she would say she needs to be left alone. She needs nothing.

Agnes from Denmark

Agnes's example highlights that it can take considerable time and sensitivity to mutually identify a therapeutic focus with people who have complex health conditions. Beyond any formal assessments, therapists will also need to gain a broader sense of the person they are working with – who they are, what they hope for, and how they see their needs.

COMMUNICATION STYLE

Closely linked to the clients' level of health complexity are their communication style and abilities. When working with clients who do not have conventional forms of communication, the therapist is often guided by non-verbal and musical responses within the therapy experiences. To explain how the client directs the therapeutic focus, Carol from the USA said:

[The client, well], they participate, they don't participate, they try, they don't try... They certainly let you know if an objective that you've put into place is contrary to what they are willing to even take part in, in their own health. So the client pretty much directs everything. At which time then we have to go back to the drawing board and figure out what other objectives can we put in place here.

Carol from the USA

Taking this further, Sarah, a researcher and clinician in neonatal care, added to Carol's reflection about the client communicating their wishes non-verbally by explaining:

I mean from my work, a ten-week-old baby can control the session. I show [students] the footage of the baby completely leading the session with me, and me trying desperately hard to be the therapist and the baby, you know, they're clearly saying 'stop that's enough', you know, 'go away', and all those sorts of things, which makes [the students] roar with laughter, but actually it is a very salient lesson for them. And so yeah, absolutely client-centred.

Sarah from the USA

Similarly, people who can communicate with speech and text can nonetheless have difficulty expressing what they want to focus on in music therapy. Some people can only express their desires for music therapy in broad terms. In reflecting on his work with people at a community mental health service, Timothy from Australia explains:

> Usually [the person identifies] something like 'to meet people', or 'to learn how to play music'. Sometimes you'll get people saying something more therapeutic like 'because I've got anxiety'.

Timothy from Australia

Other interviewees described how sometimes the people they work with seem to feel compelled to quickly identify a focus for the therapy, and then feel that they are obligated to stick with the goal they first articulated. This situation is reminiscent of Lee Child's 'plotter' approach (Kanowski, 2018), where goals set at the commencement of therapy could make someone feel 'straitjacketed'. I explored this concept further in the interview with Jarle from Norway:

Jarle: And then, of course, you would have instances where, which was probably for me the most challenging to contain, if [the person] would...stick to the one goal and never change it. And [the challenge is when] my interpretation is that this goal is perhaps a bit narrow.

Thompson: So...are there times, then, that the goal itself can become the expert almost, or...imposing something on the process?

Jarle: Absolutely. I mean, I really do think that goals affect what you do. Not in any kind of direct way because you do things for many reasons, and there are so many layers and...but the goals are part of the process.

UNDERSTANDING OF MUSIC THERAPY

Following on, many participants acknowledged that the level of understanding a person has about music therapy in the first place will greatly impact their ability to collaborate in goal processes. If music therapy is not well understood, articulating or indicating what they hope to gain from the experience becomes fraught. The participants described the way some people respond to their uncertainty about the focus for music therapy as a tendency to identify a *music experience* they would like to engage in, rather than being clear about the *purpose*. The quotes below provide a snapshot of some of these descriptions.

> Even though it's called 'music therapy' people don't always necessarily know that it's therapy. So in [my context], I also think of therapy, and of each music experience, as an opportunity. So here I've got a couple of opportunities: we can improvise on that concept, we can compose about that concept, or maybe we have a song in mind that helps us look at that idea.

Mark from the USA

> [Sometimes the person] doesn't understand what music therapy is, and they think they are having piano lessons or something like that, and then, you know, there is also a process of explaining 'what could this be?' And give them some experiences so they could develop the goals together. What is possible here? Because sometimes you meet clients that have never had this kind of experience before, that music could be used this way.

Luna from Denmark

[The young people in hospital] knew I made music. They knew that, you know, something great happened here. They heard it from a friend or that, you know. So I never once had somebody come to me to say they wanted to work on something other than being in a music relationship with me. They never said, 'I want to cope with being in the hospital.'

Jake from the USA

Sometimes [the person/s] would have concrete goals of 'we want to write a song about World AIDS Day and use it as advocacy and let people know that they are not alone.' And to me, it's more natural with the client that they sort of decide method first.

Rebecca from Norway

When someone comes into something new, they are totally reliant on the leader, you know, which is the therapist, to tell them and show them and model to them 'this is what we do and how we do it and why', all of those things. And if at the beginning the therapist sits back and just leaves it all up to the client...then the client is uncomfortable.

Timothy from Australia

When the people music therapists work with find it easier to identify a music experience they would like to engage in, this should not be seen as an inferior approach. I also don't see it quite the same as Bruscia's 'experience-oriented' approach (Bruscia, 2014), since the music therapy method is articulated early on, in a similar way as a predetermined goal would be. The person is saying, 'I want to achieve/experience/do...this.' Therefore, within this theory, the person's preference to articulate what they want as a music-based experience simply needs to be acknowledged as a factor that will impact on the way goal processes unfold. For example, Astrid describes the way her work with an adolescent in the Norwegian special education context unfolded:

> Some [clients] can reflect actually about what they want to learn. Because that's easier for them to connect to: What am I going to learn here [in music therapy], instead of what am I going to achieve? The personal development [goal] is quite difficult for them to see. But they have thoughts upon what they want to learn. [I worked with one] very shy girl who said she wanted to sing a song at the summer concert. [I thought] it was a crazy goal actually because she was not there at all. But we spent a year practising. She wouldn't sing in the microphone even. And then she tried to make some sounds in the microphone, and then [I asked her], 'Oh what kind of songs do you want to sing?' And we found songs on YouTube and we practised and practised. And when the summer concert, the date for the summer concert gradually got closer, we went to look at the stage and we were talking about how many people there would be. And she actually did it! She sang in the microphone for 200 people. Yes! It's still...I can't believe that she actually did it, but we worked towards that specific goal that she herself was part of setting.

Astrid from Norway

Through respectful interactions, accepting where the person wants to start and acknowledging the person's emphasis on music experiences, the therapist can help the person they are working with to understand these music experiences as a domain of health and wellbeing. Doing so may open up different possibilities for the next phase of work together, since these music experiences can emphasize the mutual and shared creative opportunities in the sessions.

As the person's musicality deepens and expands, the therapist can respectfully invite the person to try other possibilities when the time is right. For example, Jarle from Norway continued to reflect on his role as therapist when the people he worked with wanted to keep going with one goal and never change it. He explains:

[If a person says] 'I want to use music for relaxation. Full Stop.' If [the person] stays there, and if my interpretation would be that perhaps there are other options here and possibilities too, how do you know how to...acknowledge and recognize that person's choice, and at the same time try to see if and when and how I should point in other directions? To find that balance of respecting the person's choice and helping them see other possibilities. That was...sometimes challenging. And there could be other examples where the person could have goals which, in my appraisal, are not the most helpful goal here. Like...patients struggling with aggression and having the idea that they could get rid of aggression by drumming loudly. Which...rarely seems to work in my experience. But then again, we need to kind of have that process and make that experience, and have that conversation and the negotiation going. So...it's not an easy way of working, I feel. It kind of...requires that you really work with trust; you work with communication and relationship. And it requires kind of...that you work on quite a few levels with that person to make it fruitful.

Jarle from Norway

Jarle's example highlights how 'outcome' and 'process' cannot be easily separated. Even when a clear outcome is identified early on, the therapist is dynamically inviting the person they work with to consider other ways of being and supporting them to deepen their understanding of music for health and wellbeing.

Invitation to reflexivity: Think about a person you have worked with recently and reflect on how they communicated what they wanted to do, or what they wanted to focus on in music therapy. Were they more likely to focus on the music method (e.g. song singing) or a non-musical health outcome? How did you articulate the goal for this person?

LEVEL OF ENGAGEMENT

So far, we have considered the impact of the initial referral themes, the person's health complexity, their communication style, and their degree of understanding of music therapy on the therapeutic focus. Intertwined with these factors is the person's level of engagement, in terms of both how they perceive the role of music in their life and their overall motivation for entering into a therapy process.

The participants made various observations and reflections about how the person's level of engagement might impact the goal process. Some themes overlap with assessment considerations, such as trying to determine what really motivates and sparks interest for the person we are working with. Amy from Australia, explains:

> I suppose what I'm most interested in is what the...what the student or person I'm working with is... What they're into, you know? What kind of turns them on and gives them motivation and... You know, I'm interested in who they are and what's going to kind of spark their interest and their motivation. So I suppose I'm most interested in that, to begin with. And then I see in terms of the goals in music therapy, I'm looking for the ways in which I can support that, whatever their interest might be.

Amy from Australia

In situations where people might have low motivation to engage in therapy, identifying a focus for the work may feel like a struggle. In this situation, participants were hesitant to decide on goals right at the beginning as they risk being meaningless at best or oppressive at worst. Therefore, the person's sense of agency and ownership around their therapeutic goals was viewed as vital for many of the participants in this research. Fostering agency is relevant whether goals need to be predetermined or could be more emergent, and the complexity was acknowledged by many of the participants. Reflecting on music-centred approaches where the therapist and the person they work with are co-creating and mutually invested in the music experience, Theo from the USA explained:

> We co-create something; the agency was from within as opposed to a mechanism from without. So the tricky part in goal writing, goal language, is: how do you write 'opportunity'? How do you write... how do you keep the agency with the agent as opposed to with the mechanism?

Theo from the USA

The deep respect and consideration for the person runs much deeper, it seems, than simply completing an assessment and writing a goal or the therapist deciding to let the process unfold through the music experiences offered or suggested. These participants highlight the rich and dynamic partnership between the therapist and client, which implies an ethics of practice that might challenge the therapist's preferred theoretical approach. Similarly, engaging with the client in the spirit of partnership might also frustrate the system that demands an up-front goal before funding will be approved. Julia from Scotland told this powerful story in her interview to highlight the pressure she experienced from the system as she attempted to work in partnership with her client in a community adult mental health context:

So, I was working with one person, a very intelligent young man. I spent ages not setting goals with him because I knew it was going to be a problem, and I knew that it was not something that would come easily. But there are certain constraints; I do have to eventually give some feedback to the team. So I said to [this young man], 'We have to start thinking about where we're going with this.' I don't think I would have used the term 'goal setting' with him... So we have a chat, and then I said, 'Well, maybe I'll write this down.' And he said to me, 'Oh, yeah, I'd love to see some creative writing', and he laughed. And I just thought, that's my writing, isn't it? It's not your writing. So actually, we're in this space where he feels that people keep doing things for him and keep making stories which don't quite fit.

Julia from Scotland

Reflecting on the attributes of the people we work with can help to illuminate deeper understanding of goal processes. Each person is unique, and so by reflecting on specific situations and the individual's attributes, an opportunity for insight into barriers and enablers can emerge for the therapist. Worksheet 2 invites you to map out your own reflections related to the attributes of one of the individuals or groups that you work with (see Appendix).

The next chapter will reflect the context as an important real-world consideration in therapy work. The interdependence of each player within this model continues to be deliberated by delving into the impact of the context on both the therapist and the person/s they work with.

REFERENCES

Bruscia, K.E. (2014). *Defining Music Therapy* (3rd edn). New Braunfels, TX: Barcelona Publishers.

Kanowski, S. (2018). What Jack Reacher did next [Audio podcast episode]. In *Conversations with Richard Fidler, Sarah Kanowski*. ABC, 30 November. Accessed on 3/11/2021 at www.abc.net.au/radio/programs/conversations/lee-child-2018/10551066

CHAPTER 6

Features of the context

The context has a powerful role to play within goal processes, with flow-on ethical considerations. Therapists need to be well prepared to navigate these issues, and well supported to conceptualize their work within contexts that have a tight scope of practice. Where therapists are unprepared for the impact the context can have on their work, they may slide into oppressive practices (Baines, 2012, 2021) or become dissatisfied and burnt-out.

The work context can also provide important boundaries on the quality and nature of the therapist–client relationship.[1] We are traditionally more accustomed to thinking about the primacy of the intimate relationship between therapist and client within therapy training, exemplified by the philosophical stance of one of the early humanistic therapists, Irvin Yalom (2017):

> What is important in therapy is the here and now relationship between therapist and client. You have to be open to invent a therapy for each client rather then apply a technique or theory such as in traditional psychoanalysis. The mutative force in therapy is not intellectual insight, not interpretation, not catharsis, but is, instead, a deep, authentic meeting between two people. (Chapter 30)

---

1   The therapist–client relationship may also be expanded to include the family or the immediate team working with a particular person, or to think about group work as its own microcosm of society.

Yalom's description of the therapist–client relationship conjures an image of the two existing in their own private bubble. Striving towards an authentic meeting between two people within the 'here-and-now' moments of the session is, perhaps, a type of meta-goal for the therapist who aligns with a humanistic framework. However, as Julia's reflection highlighted at the end of the previous chapter, the employment context creates certain expectations, pressures, and affordances. If therapists fail to acknowledge the impact of the context, there is a risk of disassociating our work from the forces at play in the broader social system. I find Yalom's stance intoxicatingly attractive, yet it requires the philosophy of both the context and therapist to deeply align. For example, Astrid from Norway described her work within a special school setting where her own humanistic stance perfectly aligned with the school's expectations for music therapy:

> In some school settings, I also have [worked with] some wonderful teachers that [have said to me], 'This pupil. He doesn't master anything really, so we just want him to have music therapy where I can feel that he's mastering something. Forget about every goal. Just let him feel that he can achieve something that...something that makes him happy.' And [for me] that's a perfect starting point. One of the [other] teachers said to me, 'I have this boy in my class. He's so little inside that he's almost invisible. Can you give him music therapy?'. I said, 'Yes, of course!'

Astrid from Norway

Astrid's experience of working in this special school reveals the presence of a third player in goal processes: the context. Consider what might have happened if Astrid had said to the teacher who told her to 'forget every goal' for the young person that this was not appropriate for music therapy. Alternatively, consider the impact on practice if Astrid felt trivialized by being asked to focus her sessions on 'just something that makes the client happy'. Based on the interview data and grounded theory analysis, the degree to which the therapist and client relate to each other is very much influenced by the context in which they meet. However, the ways in which the context impacts goal processes is often not communicated, with the exception being within the anti-oppressive practice discourse (Baines, 2012, 2021; Scrine, 2021) that deeply acknowledges the range of systemic harms that can occur in therapy practices.

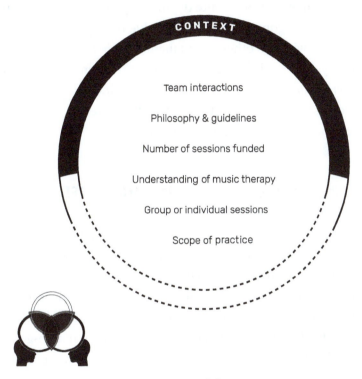

CONTEXT

Team interactions

Philosophy & guidelines

Number of sessions funded

Understanding of music therapy

Group or individual sessions

Scope of practice

Figure 6.1: Features of the context

The client-in-context theory proposes that the features of the employment context have a strong bearing on the process of identifying a therapeutic focus. Some contexts have a clearly defined *philosophy and guidelines* that lead to a definitive *scope of practice*. This means that people receiving services within a highly regulated context will often be seen to have similar needs and expectations for therapy outcomes. The way therapy services are funded within a context will also impact the therapeutic focus. Some contexts will have strict regulations around the *number of sessions funded*, or whether *group/individual sessions* can be provided. Further, different contexts will have differing *team interactions* due to their size and composition, such as large multidisciplinary teams, small transdisciplinary teams, or an individual therapist's private practice. The way the team interacts, and the degree of autonomy of team members that is possible within a context, similarly impacts the therapeutic focus. Some contexts will highly value or require collaborative approaches, while, in others, team members operate relatively independently. The employers' expectations for outcomes and their level of *understanding of music therapy* as a discipline will also influence the process of identifying a therapeutic focus (see Figure 6.1). Each of these categories is further elaborated below.

PHILOSOPHY AND GUIDELINES

As explicated by Astrid's example above, the philosophy of the employment context will likely have a powerful bearing on the ways goals are identified and articulated. Theo from the USA described that each setting has its own 'ecology of care'. During the interviews, the music therapists reflected on times where their own philosophy or theoretical framework was either a 'good fit' or 'not-so-good fit' with their employment context. Luna from Denmark explained:

> Sometimes you need to adapt your own language, even though you...believe in other theories, you need actually...you need to acquaint yourself with the language used in this place. And try to...translate your ideas. [For example], I've been working in a clinic with cognitive behavioural therapy, and actually it was a nice challenge because I found out that this was a nice way to develop new concepts about how music and feelings could go together; how I could educate about feelings with music.

Luna from Denmark

Luna's description of how she adapts her language and tries to translate her ideas to align better with the philosophy of her work context is important. It is logical that therapists will make these adaptions and translations; however, the ease with which the therapist can do so is worth further consideration. In the next section, I will highlight some of the insights offered by the participants related to particular contexts.

Reflections on school contexts

Music therapists working in school settings acknowledged that their work needed to align with the young person's individualized plan[2] since this is generated by the team and reflects the guidelines and philosophy of the education system. Julia from Scotland described that her music therapy practice must focus on 'support for learning' and 'removing barriers to learning'. Julia expressed that her work must be 'squeezed into that box to stay at the table'. This sentiment was echoed by others too, who felt that they needed to frame their work according to the employment context in order to keep their job. There is a sense of ethical tension here that underpins the therapist's descriptions of settings when they do not feel perfectly aligned with the philosophy of the setting.

Beyond the young person's individualized plan, schools typically have a curriculum framework that provides further guidelines for practice. For example, the school leadership team may consider that music therapy is particularly well suited to supporting social capabilities within the curriculum for special education, and therefore goals will focus on relational behaviours and skills. Amy from Australia explained that she moves between thinking about 'the curriculum, to the teachers' goals for a student, and then...the music therapy goals grow from that after a few sessions'.

---

2   There are various terms used, such as 'coordinated support plans', 'individualized education plans (IEPs)', etc.

Reflections on government policies and funding schemes

Some countries have broad health policies that define the nature of the work that will be funded. The participants from countries such as Australia, England, Scotland, Denmark, and Norway made particular mention of the impact that these funding schemes have on their goal processes. Their reflections provide a powerful insight into the way that the therapist–client relationship shifts relative to broader societal movements. When Amy from Australia started to describe her work in the context of being funded by the National Disability Insurance Scheme (NDIS),[3] I asked her who the goal is for, and what is its function? Amy replied:

> For my NDIS work, it's about how to ensure...how to use the NDIS language to ensure that we have further funding for our work, if that's what's needed. And so I say that [the goals] are directed towards the NDIS planner. That's probably foremost in my mind when I'm thinking about writing the goal and writing it as part of reports. But it's not that I ignore the person I'm working with at all, and I have their goals in my mind as well.

Amy from Australia

As indicated previously, the therapist needs to be pragmatic to a certain degree in order to keep their job. Freja from Denmark takes a realistic approach and explains that goals must meet both the clients' and the society's needs:

---

3   See Chapter 2 for more details about the NDIS and other forms of government funding.

Goals have to be linked to all the levels in the model in order to meet both the client's need, the professional knowledge of music therapy, and the society's need when taxes are paying for effective treatment.

Freja from Denmark

Both Amy and Freja openly acknowledge the constraints placed on them by the system. However, there are also times where guidelines and policies are ambivalent in nature. For example, various funding guidelines outline restrictions for services while simultaneously stating the importance of patient choice and control. Jarle from Norway considers that while therapists may need to adapt their practice to better align with policy, they should at the same time seriously seek to use democratic and empowering possibilities to work creatively within the system:

[Health policy] here...has been formalized in a way which stresses patient choice. Which then has led to the development [and consideration] of 'How could we improve the processes where actually patients take part?' [The patient] can then negotiate about goals... So there's a kind of whole process of change now, where [the patient] has this right to participate in the decision-making, it's simply called 'shared decision-making'.

Jarle from Norway

Reflections on brief therapy approaches

A number of the therapists I interviewed worked in settings where they may only have one or very few sessions with an individual or group. In medical settings, this feature of the work was well understood, and therefore the philosophy of practice required goals to be considered in a particular way. Some respondents were comfortable with this model, understanding that focusing on the here-and-now was appropriate and practical. Brigit from Norway described her work in a paediatric hospital setting:

> It is the same process, but it is just quicker. So we meet the patient, and we have to really think fast: what can I do for this person? What can we create together that will be good for this patient or a family or their brothers and sisters? And then we do something together, and then I evaluate, and I write a note in the patient's journal about what happened. And maybe I will meet them three times or maybe...some patients I only meet one time.

Brigit from Norway

As an experienced therapist, Brigit understands that facilitating single sessions demands a distinct approach to the way she thinks about goal processes. The therapist will likely consider the person's here-and-now needs, the referral themes, the team's scope of practice, and their knowledge of the person's condition all at the same time. The therapist may have an overarching set of goals to guide their practice, which are then refined and documented after the session.

SCOPE OF PRACTICE

The philosophy of a particular context is typically linked to the scope of practice. For example, people come to a school to receive an education and go to a hospital for medical treatment. While the philosophy may encompass a broader expectation for the way services are provided within a particular context, a scope of practice is often precisely defined. Therapists working in these settings might consider that they have developed a specialization in the field. Several interviewees reflected on how their work in specialized contexts significantly impacted their goal processes. The following sub-sections bring together participants' reflections on how the workplace scope of practice impacts the therapeutic focus.

Specialist treatment settings

In certain workplaces, the term 'treatment' is fitting, since the context brings together a team of experts to address the needs of specific health conditions. People might be admitted as in-patients or out-patients, and they give consent for a particular form of specialist care. Music therapists who work within these contexts may be employed to address very specific aspects of the patients' treatment within the organization's scope of practice, with the employment agreement being the dominant driver of the focus for music therapy. George from England powerfully explained the rationale behind his approach to goal processes in neurorehabilitation:

> We know that change can be induced in the brain, and the way that the brain is connected, in a short period of time. There are [short] windows of opportunity. So, I'm not necessarily going to go with the patient saying [to me], 'I don't really feel like doing it today.' To put it very simply, I [believe doing this therapy is] for your own benefit. You have the potential to recover a lot more... We've got [a limited number of sessions] to do what you need. And I want you to get enough of what you need.

George from England

George goes on to explain that the patient's goals are set by the rehabilitation team, and all therapy services must align with these. When I interviewed George, I could feel that he was passionate about his work and there was a strong alignment between his own theoretical frameworks and the scope of practice of the neurorehabilitation setting he worked in. George's sentiments were supported by other music therapists describing their own work in medical settings where the goals are very much determined by the context or the team. For example, therapists working in specialized medical units are likely to work with clients with very similar symptoms or concerns. Andre from the USA explained how his work in a radiology and oncology ward means that his practice focuses mostly on symptom management such as state anxiety and depression, and therefore his goals are 'pretty clear-cut' and 'not something I'd usually negotiate with patients'.

Specialized funding agreements

Settings can also be shaped around funding criteria that narrowly define the scope of practice. Patsy from the USA reflected on her early work in a psychiatric setting. She remembers applying for the job, and the interviewer said to her:

> Things have changed. There's no more psychotherapy, no more psychodynamic [approach]. You're going to be teaching coping skills, because the insurance companies run the show. And you are going to see people for [only] one or two sessions, so teach them.

Patsy from the USA

Patsy went on to explain that the music therapy goals were more or less predetermined by the funding agreement's emphasis on stress, anxiety, and anger management skills.

Other therapists reflected on the pressure that predetermined goals create in their practice, particularly if the person they are working with does not seem to be making progress. Jennifer from England expressed concern about funding being jeopardized if the person does not show progress in specific ways. Cathy from Italy was concerned that her program would not be valued if the outcomes were different from those expected. Similarly, Amy from Australia explained that she needs to write goals with functional outcomes that can be observed and measured in order to retain her contract to work with people with disability even though she does not feel these goals accurately portray the work. From his vantage point as a senior practitioner, Theo from the USA could better understand the struggles he faced in his early career, explaining:

> I was doing my best in those days to...I guess [I was trying to] assimilate into the contexts. [This was] long before I felt like I had an independent identity as a music therapist, which took years really for me to feel it; for that to settle in. And so there were times when...I felt like I had to play a game. But a game in the sense of 'do what the system was expecting of me'.

Theo from the USA

NUMBER OF SESSIONS FUNDED

The practical aspects of a particular context also have a significant impact on goal processes, and subsequently flow on to the way therapy is planned and facilitated. Mary from Scotland describes how tariff-based therapy models have necessitated a change in the way she approaches goal processes:

> I've really challenged myself over the years because we've had to become really much tighter in how we deliver our work. Gone are the days where you can work with someone for five, six years and...you know, be justified. 'Cause [now] I don't even think that's necessarily helpful anyway. For some people, ten weeks actually is enough, and it feels...quite neat in a way. It feels as if actually it's been enough to help that person move on.

Mary from Scotland

GROUP OR INDIVIDUAL SESSIONS

Some settings emphasize group work over individual work within the scope of practice. Group work can be seen to be a more suitable approach to address the needs of people who access that service, and/or more efficient use of funding. The interviewees working within group therapy models reflected in various ways about how this approach impacted their goal processes. Timothy from Australia explained his approach as follows:

> When you're doing a group, it's a little bit different, because you can't change the group for [an individual] person so much. So you have to decide in advance what the goals are, and you sort of promote the group around what the group is about and trying to achieve. And so you refer into the group for people that you think might have those needs. So it's a little bit of a flip. Instead of defining it, what are the needs, and then deciding on the goals, you decide on the goals and then you search for the person with that need. Broadly [in community mental health] the goals are really relational goals. Because you're using a group. So it's about people feeling more comfortable and effective and valued and those sorts of things.

Timothy from Australia

Following on, another feature of the group context that impacts goal process is when a group has a changing membership. Rosemary from the USA explained how she supported her students to understand how to approach goal process with these types of groups:

When I would work clinically in psychiatry, and students would come in and see that I only know two people, and there are eight people [in the group]. [The students would ask me], 'How do you know what your goals are?' And I would say, so the first music experience we do, we're looking at things like what is the energy level, who's able to relate to whom, do we have people who are going to be very high or disruptive, or people who are very depressed, [and] how is all of this working together? And then, therefore, how can we create music experiences that are going to let each one of these people meet their goals. And we'll deal with those objectives or goals as the person is responding to us.

Rosemary from the USA

TEAM INTERACTIONS

Some of the research participants described how their interactions with colleagues impact their goal processes and practice. Working collegially was considered by some to be part of their practice ethics, since they incorporate a 'team lens' to their goal processes. Others spoke about the importance of a 'common vision', which then helped them to zone in on a specific area within music therapy sessions. When they contribute to team meetings, music therapists saw value in sharing their distinct perspectives. Astrid from Norway stated:

It's important for me that I don't work with goals or towards goals that are isolated; for me, it makes more sense that we all work differently towards the same goals.

Astrid from Norway

Paolo from Italy used a poetic metaphor to explain the great value he sees in sharing multiple perspectives within team collaborations:

> Within multidisciplinary work, one approach is that, when various professions meet together, that might be a level where the goal [can benefit from the] various ingredients. For example, when a poet goes to a forest, he sees the forest and the trees with the eyes of a poet. If a carpenter goes to the forest, he sees a chair, a table. So this difference of perspective, and integrating [each of] them and respecting them, can create an all-around vision of the person in that case.

Paolo from Italy

These two perspectives highlight the importance of integration and complementarity within teamwork. The therapeutic relationship therefore must be considered within the context in order for goals to be relevant and meaningful.

THE TEAM'S UNDERSTANDING OF THE MUSIC THERAPY PROFESSION

Alongside the impact of team interactions on goal processes, the level of understanding about music therapy within the team can also play a role in the way goals are determined. Within this theme, the interviewees reflected more on times when they believed the breadth of music therapy practice was not well understood in a particular context and described the challenges this lack of understanding created for them.

For example, Theo from the USA described moments in his career where the setting understood music therapy more mechanistically than relationally. Theo's understanding of music therapy as an intersubjective dialogical process was difficult for colleagues in some settings to appreciate. He reflected:

The language of 'it works' is what I feel governs a lot of our thinking about goals. There's a mechanism. There's this mechanism somewhere, whatever it is, that is true, and it has a way of working. And our job is to tap into the mechanism and manipulate it properly with technical skill, we're technicians. And if we do that correctly, the outcomes will be as desired or statistically, predictably enough, you know? So that even though no one says that out loud, that's the currency. That's where the capital is.

In my current identity [as a music therapist], and thinking about goals, it's not 'it works', it's 'we work' or 'I work', being the client, you know? And so it's an intersubjective dialogue; [a] dialogical process, not a monological objective process. I think you asked me, 'What does [being] music centred mean?' To me, [mechanistic thinking] is in conflict with the core nature of music itself. To put music in the category of a mechanism is to only use the term 'music' as a word, but substantively to deny its existence.

Theo from the USA

Samantha, also from the USA, is an expert in rehabilitation settings. Similar to Theo, Samantha described her challenges with the way music therapy was understood by her colleagues and junior practitioners:

The reality of working in rehabilitation, is just that it's very...problem oriented. Patient-oriented, but a problem-oriented approach to setting goals, and how important that is, but it doesn't mean it's easy. I always struggled with it, all the time. And I was teaching younger clinicians to try and work in a goal-oriented setting when they hadn't necessarily trained that way. And that was a real struggle, and it was a struggle for me as well. It's a real struggle to...even if you identify the goal, how are you actually going to go about meeting that? Particularly if you're using a very music-centred approach...how do you go about it?

Samantha from the USA

The struggles and tensions described related to the features of the work context further highlight the importance of reflective practice. When a practitioner feels this sense of tension or struggle, pausing to reflect on the restrictions placed on practice by contextual factors may lead to new insights. Worksheet 3 invites you to map out your own reflections related to the features of your workplace (see Appendix).

The conditions created by each of these three entities (the therapist, the client, and the context) interact together in complex ways that create various consequences for the process of identifying the therapeutic focus. The therapist must interact with both the client and the context. The client must interact with both the therapist and the context. The context creates the opportunity for the client and therapist to interact, but also imposes a degree of structure on the way that interaction can take place. The next chapter will explore the interactions between each of the players and the theoretical consequences that various conditions might have on goal processes.

REFERENCES

Baines, S. (2012). Music therapy as an anti-oppressive practice. *The Arts in Psychotherapy 40*(1), 1–5. Accessed on 3/11/2021 at https://doi.org/10.1016/j.aip.2012.09.003

Baines, S. (2021). Anti-oppressive music therapy: Updates and future considerations. *The Arts in Psychotherapy 75*, 1–5. Accessed on 3/11/2021 at https://doi.org/10.1016/j.aip.2021.101828

Scrine, E. (2021). The limits of resilience and the need for resistance: Articulating the role of music therapy with young people within a shifting trauma paradigm. *Frontiers in Psychology 12*, 1–12. Accessed on 3/11/2021 at https://doi.org/10.3389/fpsyg.2021.600245

Yalom, I. (2017). *Becoming Myself: A Psychiatrist's Memoir*. New York, NY: Basic Books.

CHAPTER 7

Interactions between the players

The previous chapters have described each of the players in a fairly separate way. However, as indicated by the diagram representing the client-in-context model, the attributes of each player are expected to influence each other, and, in turn, these interactions further influence the therapeutic focus. In this chapter, the interactions *between* each combination of players will be elaborated.

BETWEEN THE THERAPIST AND THE CLIENT: THE THERAPEUTIC ALLIANCE

According to the APA *Dictionary of Psychology*, 'therapeutic alliance' is:

> a cooperative working relationship between client and therapist, considered by many to be an essential aspect of successful therapy. Derived from the concept of the psychoanalytic working alliance, the therapeutic alliance comprises *bonds*, *goals*, and *tasks*. Bonds are constituted by the core conditions of therapy, the client's attitude toward the therapist, and the therapist's style of relating to the client; *goals* are the mutually negotiated, understood, agreed upon, and regularly reviewed aims of the therapy; and *tasks* are the activities

carried out by both client and therapist. (American Psychological Association, 2020; emphasis added)

This definition emphasizes that goal processes are integral to the therapeutic alliance, with the quality of cooperation, negotiation, attitudes, and relationship all contributing to the 'success' of therapy. As discussed in Chapter 5, clients' attributes will substantially impact the style, degree, and nature of cooperation and negotiation. The sheer breadth of practice areas for music and creative arts therapists, which include working with people across the spectrums of age, communication styles, levels of consciousness, levels of insight, and neurological differences, intersect to shape the therapeutic alliance. For example, a person might be excited to sing or play instruments, and the therapists' style of relating to them successfully motivates their musical participation, but the person may be unable to negotiate or understand the therapeutic goals for the work.

The strength of the therapeutic alliance is therefore a key factor in *how* the therapeutic focus is determined. Further, the codes and themes derived from the interview data indicated that it is the *level of collaboration* possible with each person that is an important determinant of the strength of the therapeutic alliance. Where a person's health and communication are such that they can actively participate in the process of determining the focus of the therapy, many of the therapists interviewed saw this as optimal and believed the collaboration would lead to more effective therapy. The way the therapist attempts to collaborate draws on their values and beliefs, as well as their theoretical influences. Some therapists also described a potential to risk the therapeutic alliance if these collaborations inadvertently put the person under pressure due to their poor health or level of cognition. One of the therapists interviewed highlighted the importance of continuously engaging in 'disciplined subjectivity', while many others emphasized their commitment to ethical reflexivity. Some interviewees explained the ways they weigh up the risk of taking power over the direction of the therapy with empathically recognizing there are times when the therapist must take the lead.

Level of collaboration

Fostering mutual negotiation within therapy sessions calls for therapists to be empathic while acknowledging their professional responsibility for the quality of the working relationship. Agnes from Denmark described how she explains this responsibility very carefully to music therapy students:

[Students in training] have to use themselves as a kind of tool; to sense and to be empathic, and to know what are the needs of the clients. But on the other hand, as soon as it is in any way possible, they need to check out with the client, 'Is this okay for you? Is this okay that I do this, I play this way, or that we work in this way, is this okay for you?'

Agnes from Denmark

Freja, also from Denmark, considers this responsibility in a slightly different way by focusing on the therapist finding balance in their role if they only 'follow' the client. She explains:

[The therapist] might be even too 'client-centred', you know, always following, following, following...and I would say, 'Stop a moment. You have to show the clients what they can use music therapy to do.' So if [the therapist] just follows, follows, follows...the clients will never know how they can use the music, or use you. So, sometimes [the therapist] has to say, 'Okay, I'm showing you a little bit more.'

Freja from Denmark

Some of the music therapists interviewed described specific factors that particularly influence the therapeutic alliance and the flow-on impact on goal processes. These factors were grouped into three broad themes: working with verbally articulate people, working with minimally verbal people, and working with groups. Each of these circumstances will be discussed below.

Working with verbally articulate people

In this circumstance, the possibility for collaboration and negotiation in the goal process is high. There was a real sense of enthusiasm in the way therapists described their interactions with articulate people, noting that some people 'would actually really grab this possibility' to negotiate. Many interviewees described their style of relating to their client with respect and empathy through gentle and warm inquiries such as 'Where do we begin?' or 'What can we do in here that might be helpful for you?' or 'What do you want to achieve? What do you want to focus on here? What's important to you?' or 'Why do *you* think you are coming to music therapy?'

Clara from Denmark further explained the importance of the therapist's role within the negotiation. She felt this was particularly the case when clients articulate their desire to focus on a music experience:

> If [the person] says 'I really love to make songs' or 'I really like to sing' or 'I love the piano. I love the drums', [the therapist should say], 'Great. Let's work.' You [the therapist] have to choose [the focus of the goals]. Well, we'll use the songs and the song writing, so maybe let's start with this as some of the things we will do together.

Clara from Denmark

Clara's approach is highly transparent in the sense that the therapist's role is clearly articulated to the person they are working with during the negotiation of the therapeutic focus. Clara also described how she encourages the person to be part of the reporting and evaluation of the goals, which in her view takes goal processes to 'the next level' of mutual negotiation.

Working with minimally verbal people

There are many reasons why a person may have difficulty verbally expressing themselves, such as speech and language impairments, age, disability, trauma, or simply having a quiet personality. The music therapists interviewed described various ways that they offered opportunities for collaboration and negotiation with people who are minimally verbal. With children, some therapists offered a choice of topics and experiences, and explained what other children have done in music therapy. Other music therapists talked about empathically following the child's interests and preferences initially, but then openly negotiating future steps by saying something like 'I think we should do this now. How about we…?' Bronwyn from Scotland explained the delicate balance in negotiating with children and young people:

> So [we are] in relationship. It wasn't just that I would follow whatever they were doing…it was responsive. And it wasn't completely directionless, because I wouldn't just leave them with not knowing what to do. Because I think that's a really strange situation for them as well. So it would depend on where they were in the relationship, and how much direction they needed. And I guess, if I was adding a bit of direction, it was coming from a place of an aim. Of thinking 'Let's try something new' or 'Let's try this'. So the aims were in my mind: using music as a means for them to explore and reflect and express themselves.

Bronwyn from Scotland

Music therapists working with minimally verbal people in disability services described the way the team and family negotiate the therapeutic focus on the person's behalf. While the music therapists acknowledged that they were attentive to the here-and-now interactions with disabled people, they felt more needed to be done to actively include the person in negotiating the direction of the therapy. They considered that negotiation with the disabled person was most challenging, or most overlooked, in situations where the person had very limited means to express themselves.

Therapists who work in a family-centred approach with disabled people of various ages described how collaborating with family members expands the concept of the therapeutic alliance to the whole family. As a family-centred music therapist myself, I have seen first-hand the complexity of dynamics that can occur, particularly when the family identifies a goal that may be too advanced for the person with disability, or the therapist has a different view of a possible starting point. At these times I find myself striving to share my knowledge with the family, particularly around developmental sequences and matching the person's ability level. In dialogue with one of the interviewees, I described how, when I'm working with families who have young children, the parents rightly want to collaborate around the direction and the focus of their child's therapy. But then if the parents see that something is not working for their child, or their child seems to be indicating that they would prefer to do something else, it creates a moment where we all have to stop and think about what we are doing. Are we going to make this child do something, or are we going to go with the flow of what's needed right now? This moment of collaborative reflection with the family can be a powerful experience that might strengthen the therapeutic alliance and foster the family members' self-efficacy.

Working with groups

In a group setting, establishing a positive therapeutic alliance is also likely to be complex due to the number of people involved and the shifting dynamics between them. In these situations, the interviewees saw the power of having a clear group aim or purpose as the starting point for fostering the therapeutic alliance. The people in the group would be, ideally, choosing to attend because of the pre-articulated group focus, or would be referred to that group because it was compatible with previously identified goals. Starting from this point where there is already an awareness of the purpose or relevance of the group has the potential to quickly create a sense of mutual cooperation as people come together for a shared purpose. Rebecca from Norway explained further:

> I work with adults who have HIV and AIDS in a day service program. I had several groups that I was offering. For the group work, it was more: here is a group and a structure. Like a song-writing group, for example. And then the group gets to decide what we do, and what our goals within this will be. I try to create this sense of identity as a group and to bring the dynamic to, not to me as an expert with something to teach them, but more of like, what do we want from this process together and here are some possibilities. So [in the group setting] sometimes it would be quite concrete. They would have goals of 'We want to write a song about World AIDS Day and use it as advocacy and let people know that they are not alone.'

Rebecca from Norway

The verbal ability of the people we work with and working in group or individual settings are just some of the factors that may impact the quality of the therapeutic alliance and the level of collaboration that is possible within our work. Take a moment to pause and reflect on your own approach to building the therapeutic alliance, and the impact that has on goal processes.

Invitation to reflexivity: Think about a particular person you are working with and describe the ways you fostered collaboration to identify the therapeutic focus.

BETWEEN THE CLIENT AND THE
CONTEXT: AUTONOMY

In considering the interactions between the client and the context, the music therapists interviewed regarded the degree of *client auton-omy* as having an important impact on the process of identifying a therapeutic focus. As discussed in Chapter 6, goals for people who access contexts with a narrow scope of practice, such as medical settings, may need to be determined by the medical team. Here, the funding model might require that all therapists are working towards predetermined goals and objectives, and even specify the number of sessions permitted, resulting in relatively minimal input from the person. Andre from the USA describes a relatively low level of patient autonomy in an oncology setting:

> I coordinate the program, and I pretty much design the music ther-apy work in oncology. [I had to consider], what are the goals of the program going to be? And so [I focused on] symptom management. I think the idea of goals for this particular population is really straightforward in that there is a very discrete system of symp-tomatology: state anxiety, depression, things like this. I think the goals are pretty clear-cut. I don't think that that's something that I'd usually negotiate with patients. But I want to say, I do believe in the therapeutic alliance, not just a therapeutic relationship, but an alliance. But I think that that alliance is built perhaps through more indirect means than...than saying, 'Let's sit down and figure out what our goals are going to be.'

Andre from the USA

Other contexts may afford very high levels of client autonomy, such as mental health services that emphasize a person's right to choose, and private practice contexts where people self-refer. The intersec-tion between what is possible within a context's scope of practice combined with the attributes of the people we work with is therefore an important consideration in goal processes.

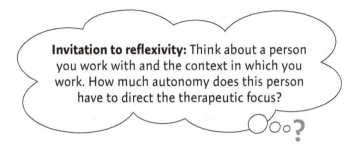

Invitation to reflexivity: Think about a person you work with and the context in which you work. How much autonomy does this person have to direct the therapeutic focus?

BETWEEN THE THERAPIST AND THE CONTEXT: PROFESSIONAL COMPATIBILITY

In considering the impact of the context, the music therapists interviewed reflected that the process of identifying the therapeutic focus was smoothest where their own values, beliefs, and theoretical framework aligned with their team, employer, or funding agency. Further, when the context has a more nuanced understanding of music therapy and the outcomes that are possible, this can lead to greater *respect* between the therapist and context, and a supportive level of *team collaboration*. This sense of compatibility and professional security creates conditions where the therapist can readily attune to the needs of the person they are working with, reflect on their knowledge base and follow their practice ethics.

Respect based on understanding

The way that an employer, funding body, or team views music therapy is likely to have a direct impact on the expectations for the focus of the music therapist's work. Assumptions can be made about what music therapy methods may be most useful for and how music therapy might support the organization's philosophy, mission, or scope of practice. Where there is a good alignment between the beliefs of the organization and the therapist, the music therapist will likely feel respected and a valuable contributor and team member. Theo from the USA experienced deep respect for creative arts therapy approaches when he worked in a cancer care setting. He recalled, 'I was given total free rein. They just said, "We just want you as a music therapist."' In contrast, Astrid from Norway struggled when working in a special education school with a behavioural approach that did not align with her more humanistic framework. While ultimately the team was open to including more relational goals in music therapy, Astrid didn't feel her work was ever fully valued. She explains:

> They probably just think it's fun, but they don't see the real value of it. I'm just that funny lady who does all this crazy stuff that just doesn't fit in with the rest of the team.

Astrid from Norway

Franco from Italy recognized the deep theoretical differences between his own professional stance and that of his medical colleagues. In Franco's home city, music therapy is informed by psychodynamic theories, but he acknowledged this made working in hospitals very complicated because the health settings align with 'behavioural or cognitive theoretical models and need quantitative goals connected with clear evidence and quantitative results'. Franco described the professional tension within him, as he recognized that the cancer care hospital understandably wanted to measure outcomes for medical symptoms such as anxiety, depression, and pain, but he valued a broader concept of care as follows:

[For me, music therapy in cancer care is also about] the quality of relationship in the group, cohesion and the opportunity to give to the patient to share emotions and feelings inside the group and with the music therapist, how the person's vision has changed related to the cancer diagnosis, the opportunity to think in a spiritual and existential way. I [therefore have to] go through this part in a deep way during my supervision process.

Franco from Italy

Team collaboration

Teams work in different ways in different contexts. There are various models for teamwork, such as multidisciplinary (or multiprofessional) where each profession works alongside each other and contributes their expert knowledge (Davis *et al.*, 2002). There are also more naturally collaborative modes such as interdisciplinary or transdisciplinary teams (King *et al.*, 2009) where professionals exchange knowledge and skills in order to work more holistically towards supporting the client's goals. Brigit from Norway explained:

When you think about goals, you have to think about the other professions you're working together with... So that we're not doing the same things as all the professionals, but we have to work together so that the patient would get what's good for them.

Brigit from Norway

Brigit's description of a relatively cohesive team environment was not always shared, particularly in teams that did not understand the music therapist's scope of practice. Some of the interviewees noted that understanding team dynamics should be part of therapy education and training. These interviewees considered that music therapy students needed encouragement to really embrace collaborative models and to understand that this is an important part of professional work. Magnus from Denmark described his view on education for music therapy students in the final stages of their training:

> [Students] need to balance the wishes from the client, their wishes as a music therapist, and the wishes from the institution.

Magnus from Denmark

Ruby from the USA similarly described the importance of teaching collaborative team models to music therapy students. She explained how, at times, students needed to be supported to let go of a more top-down or expert model and needed to do some 'mental juggling' to work with the team rather than writing goals according to protocols taught in class learning activities or copied from books.

Invitation to reflexivity: Think about one of your workplaces. How well was music therapy understood and respected by other team members? What impact did the level of professional compatibility have on the goal process?

Worksheet 4 invites you to map out your own reflections related to the intersections of each player in this theory: the therapist, the client, and the context (see Appendix). By considering the ways that these three entities interact, the client-in-context theory can be used as a powerful tool to support reflectivity and professional supervision.

In Part 3, the focus will shift to providing some practical tools for how to apply this theory to practice. Chapter 8 will use composite case examples and anecdotes from the interview data to illustrate how the theory can support deep reflection on practice and professional learning. Chapter 9 will then introduce constructive tools and guidelines for goal writing as the technical skill that underpins the goal process.

REFERENCES

American Psychological Association. (2020). Therapeutic alliance. *APA Dictionary of Psychology*. American Psychological Association. Accessed on 4/11/2021 at https://dictionary.apa.org/therapeutic-alliance

Davis, H., Day, C. & Bidmead, C. (2002). *Working in Partnership with Parents: The Parent Advisor Model*. New York, NY: Harcourt Assessment.

King, G., Strachan, D., Tucker, M., Duwyn, B., Desserud, S. & Shillington, M. (2009). The application of a transdisciplinary model for early intervention services. *Infants & Young Children 22*(3), 211–223.

PART 3

APPLICATIONS FOR PRACTICE

CHAPTER 8

The theory–practice nexus

The 'client-in-context' theory has the potential to support practice directly by inviting music and creative arts therapists to engage with the theory's broader concepts while deeply reflecting on their own specific circumstances. Moving between these two positions – a more macro level and a more micro level – offers a practical way to use this theory as part of a reflexive toolkit.

The inspiration for the theory's name comes from participants who highlighted that being 'person-centred' is important but not enough, since the people we work with are impacted by their circumstances. Stige explains: 'to claim that practice is contextual involves seeing how it is contingent (on cultural conditions, for instance) as well as connected in time and space to other practices' (2015, p.6). Perhaps the challenge of acknowledging contextuality is why so much of the literature about goals tends to focus on technical and functional aspects of goal writing. However, focusing on these technical aspects alone risks losing the relational and cultural qualities that underpin therapy practice.

In my own teaching approach, I endeavour to highlight the interplay between theoretical frameworks and contextually situated practice wisdom. Theory is understood to provide a large part of the rationale for practice, while, at the same time, practice developments can ultimately lead to the generation of new theory (Aigen, 2014; Stige, 2015). The importance of research is also emphasized in definitions of music therapy stating that practice is 'research based' (Australian Music Therapy Association), or 'evidence based' (American Music Therapy Association, 2005). It is therefore widely accepted that theory, practice, and research are interwoven (Ghetti, 2015; Stige, 2015).

The research that led to the grounded theory presented in this book invited experienced music therapists to share their insights about a very practical aspect of their work: goal setting. I invited each of the 45 participants to describe their personal experiences with identifying goals, writing goals, and teaching or supervising novice therapists to develop professional skills in goal processes. During the interviews, many participants used examples from their practice to illustrate their point or to help them find the words to explain their approach. It seemed to me that the participants were drawing on their tacit knowledge and were attempting to synthesize many aspects of their practice to respond to my interview questions and prompts. In this way, the client-in-context theory is grounded in contextually situated practice knowledge.

A key element of grounded theory analysis is the construction of an analytic paradigm that maps out different conditions and their likely interactions and consequences (Dey, 2007; Strauss & Corbin, 1998). This process can lead to the creation of short narratives that are a composite of the qualitative data to illustrate how the theory could play out. While this process remains grounded in the large data set from the study, it is also theoretically possible to apply the theory to 'new' factors that were not part of the original analysis.

In my publication of the main results from this research (Thompson, 2020), I created two composite examples where I 'imagined' a therapist with a certain set of values, who was working with a certain person in a certain context. I then theorized about the likely therapeutic focus that could ensue. Since that first publication, I have had the opportunity to present the material at conferences, workshops, and tutorials. I have had further dialogues with music therapists in different career stages about the application of this theory and the challenges they have faced in their practice when it comes to identifying and articulating their goals. What has stood out to me in these discussions is that sometimes identifying the therapeutic focus takes place quite smoothly and sometimes the process is quite fraught. The client-in-context theory highlights that there are many factors involved in goal processes, and so it stands to reason those different factors will push and pull in different directions.

In the next section, I will provide some working examples of how to apply the client-in-context theory, before offering some learning activities to enhance professionals' reflexive toolkit. I have organized the working examples into two different experiences: those that are somewhat harmonious collaborations and those that are somewhat discordant collaborations.

APPLYING THEORY TO PRACTICE: HARMONIOUS ATTRIBUTES AND FEATURES

When all of the players in this 'system' of goal process are mostly aligned, the theory highlights that identifying a therapeutic focus should flow quite well. The therapist can consider various elements and factors, and play their part in collaborating with the person they are working with, and/or the context, to write a goal in a suitable format. Two examples with somewhat harmonious working relationships are provided to illustrate the reflexive process undertaken by the hypothetical therapists.

Example 1: Ava, a music therapist working in a specialist school for autistic children

In this example, I provide a hypothetical composite case of a music therapist working in a specialist school for autistic children. The section below provides a summary of the attributes and features of each player and their intersections.

Therapist's attributes. Ava strives to maximize the client's development in various domains and works with their strengths and interests (theoretical framework). Ava wants to make sure music therapy remains relevant in the school setting and is committed to working within the curriculum framework (advocacy for profession). Ava believes that autistic children's natural forms of expression should be respected (values and beliefs) and that the child's here-and-now needs should be acknowledged (ethics of practice; comfort with flexibility). Ava has been working with autistic children for five years and understands the impact of anxiety on engagement (knowledge base).

Client's attributes. Arjan is a 10-year-old autistic boy referred to music therapy to expand his verbal and non-verbal expression (referral themes). Arjan communicates in a range of ways, including short sentences, gestures, and body language. When he doesn't want to join in with an activity, he becomes more active and walks around the room (communication style). Arjan can become anxious in loud and busy environments (health complexity). He likes Disney musicals and listens to the soundtracks on streaming services. He looks forward to sharing Disney songs with the music therapist each week (understanding of music therapy).

Features of the context. The school employs a variety of professionals and aligns with a transdisciplinary approach (team interactions). Team members are expected to collaborate and share knowledge to support student learning (philosophy and guidelines) aligned with the national curriculum (scope of work). Team members acknowledge that music experiences are highly motivating for many students at the school but many team members lack confidence to use music themselves (understanding of music therapy). The school principal believes that students are best served in their classroom groups (groups or individual sessions); this enables the budget to stretch so that students can participate in creative arts programs across the entire school year (number of sessions funded).

Therapeutic alliance (between client and therapist). Arjan often says the titles of movies and songs in the music therapy session and expects Ava the music therapist to sing the song or play the recording on her computer. Ava finds it difficult to create moments of collaboration with Arjan unless his favourite songs are being played (level of collaboration). Within group contexts, Arjan often stands up and walks over to the window when other students choose a song that he is not familiar with.

Client autonomy (between the client and the context). Within the school setting, Arjan's family and teachers create the priority for his individual education plan. Arjan's interests are respected and considered, but the team also wants to expand the repertoire of his interests where possible and support him to maximize his developmental potential.

Professional compatibility (between the therapist and the context). Music therapist, Ava, is a respected member of the team. Music therapy is considered a valuable experience and an asset to the school. The principal knows that many families choose to come to the school because it offers a high-quality creative arts program (respect). Ava broadly supports the school's commitment to developmental outcomes. There are times when Ava feels that music experiences could be better integrated into the school day beyond the music therapy sessions (team collaboration).

This hypothetical example provides a snapshot of various attributes and features that theoretically impact the therapeutic focus for Arjan. The example also highlights the volume of information and perspectives that a therapist is often required to integrate, and how mapping out various attributes and features can scaffold reflexivity.

Before reading on, think about the possible goals for Arjan in music therapy.

In this scenario, Ava is supportive of the school's scope of work and is keen to advocate for music therapy as a core service in schools, so this is a fairly harmonious collaboration. Arjan has limited opportunity to impact the broad goal domains within the school context. Given there is a good level of professional compatibility between the therapist and the context, Ava and the team might write goals and objectives for Arjan with observable outcomes that can be tracked across the year to align with the school's scope of work, philosophy, team approach, and funding agreement. Music therapy would be offered in a group context.

Possible goals and objectives

Goal: For Arjan to extend his use of language and gesture in group music experiences.

> *Rationale: compatible with Arjan's referral themes and the school's curriculum framework. Ava's stance on advocacy for the music therapy profession through alignment with the school's scope of work is supported.*

Objective 1: For Arjan to answer questions (by the music therapist or group members) about the Disney songs he shares.

> *Rationale: This objective allows for scalable and observable outcomes related to the curriculum framework. Questions for Arjan to answer can be scaffolded with pictures and gestures. Arjan can be encouraged to participate in the discussion according to his strengths and he can be gently encouraged to expand his repertoire of communication acts.*

Objective 2: For Arjan to contribute ideas to a lyric substitution of a preferred Disney song.

> *Rationale: The complexity of lyric substitution is scalable, with just one word altered to begin with. Arjan's lyric suggestions can be made through verbal responses, drawing, writing, or movement. Other group members can contribute ideas, which provides opportunity for group discussion and negotiation. The focus aligns with the curriculum framework for language development.*

Objective 3: For Arjan to ask other group members a question about their song choice.

> *Rationale: This objective allows for scalable and observable outcomes related to the curriculum framework. Arjan can ask questions in the manner he prefers, such as verbally or by selecting from a list of questions. Arjan can be gently encouraged to expand his repertoire of communication acts with more of the group members.*

Alignments and tensions for Ava, Arjan, and the school

While these suggested goals and objectives align with many of the attributes described in the hypothetical scenario, Ava should also consider the complexity described in the therapeutic alliance. Collaboration with Arjan needs to be empathically facilitated so that his interests in music are respected, along with his desire to share his interests with others in a particular way. Therefore, Ava also needs to acknowledge that Arjan can become anxious in some social contexts. The group context might increase Arjan's stress and anxiety, and so the therapist will need to consider how she can support Arjan's interests and strengths.

Given Ava's ethical position to respect the client's here-and-now needs and her comfort with flexibility, she may decide to put aside these formal goals and instead collaborate with and respond to Arjan when required. The team she works with would need to be prepared to go with the flow of any changes and provide support to Ava so that she can provide more individualized care to Arjan. While the goals themselves might not need to be altered, the manner in which Ava works towards these goals may change session to session.

In supervision, Ava might need to consider deeply the therapeutic alliance. If Arjan's here-and-now needs are often at odds with the group-based goals, Ava may feel conflicted and need support to navigate the way forward. The current professional alignment she experiences within the school context may quickly fall away if the curriculum framework ceases to feel like a good fit for Arjan. This theory also reminds us that therapy work is dynamic and that client needs are changing over time.

Example 2: Carl, a music therapist working in the oncology department of a major hospital

In this example, I provide a hypothetical composite case of a music therapist working in the oncology department of a major hospital for adult patients. The section below provides a summary of the attributes and features of each player and their intersections.

Therapist's attributes. Carl is informed by music psychotherapy and trauma theory in his work with adult oncology patients (theoretical framework). As a senior therapist, he has a clear and refined understanding of how music therapy can support symptom management (knowledge base). Carl confidently advocates for music therapy's distinct role in the oncology department and comfortably aligns with the hospital team's culture (advocacy for profession). He ensures that his patients are informed about what music therapy can offer to support common symptoms such as state anxiety and biopsychosocial pain management (ethics of practice). Carl believes that he is meeting patients at a vulnerable time in their life, and so he takes care not to over-burden them with formal negotiation of the therapeutic work (values and beliefs). Instead, the broad symptom-focused goals he has developed in collaboration with the hospital team help to ground his work as he follows the patient's lead dynamically and intuitively (comfort with flexibility).

Client's attributes. Brianna is a 52-year-old woman being treated for breast cancer. The diagnosis was a shock to her, as she works in the fitness industry and has never been admitted to hospital before (health complexity). Brianna has only heard negative stories about cancer treatment. The team observes that Brianna is restless, and although she asks a lot of questions (communication style), she seems to be struggling to understand information about her treatment plan. They refer Brianna to music therapy to manage symptoms of anxiety (referral themes). Brianna is a member of her church choir and was enthusiastic about meeting Carl the music therapist (level of engagement). She has always believed in the healing potential of music (understanding of music therapy).

Features of the context. Carl is employed at a major teaching hospital in a capital city. The oncology department offers specialized care (scope of work) and is well resourced. The team comprises physicians, nursing staff, social workers, and music therapists, and each team member is fairly autonomous and well respected (team interactions). The team shares case stories regularly, and therefore understands the strengths of each discipline (understanding of music therapy). The team believes that a combination of services results in best practice holistic care (philosophy and guidelines). As an inpatient service, team members work with patients for the duration of their hospital stay which is typically 4–6 weeks (number of sessions funded). Individual sessions are most commonly offered so that the treatment of symptoms can be carefully monitored (group or individual sessions).

Therapeutic alliance (between client and therapist). Carl gently and warmly explains to Brianna that he received a referral to visit her and introduces himself and his work. Brianna conveys that it will be great to have some help to calm down and divulges she feels worried and afraid. As Carl gently asks Brianna to tell him about herself, Brianna openly shares her musical interests, and the conversation dynamically encompasses topics about her work, family, church choir friends, and how her life has changed following the diagnosis (level of collaboration). Brianna says she is open to trying guided visualization with music.

Client autonomy (between the client and the context). Within this specialist setting, Brianna is comforted by knowing that the team members are experienced experts in the field. The team provides high-quality consultation to patients and openly answers questions. While the broad focus of music therapy is well understood as being centred around symptom management, Brianna's here-and-now psychosocial needs are respected, and the therapy process can unfold dynamically.

Professional compatibility (between the therapist and the context). The oncology team meets regularly to review patient progress and treatment (team collaboration). The psychosocial needs of the patients are recognized as being vital to good treatment outcomes. There is mutual respect and understanding between team members, and music therapy has been offered as a service for the past 20 years (respect).

Before reading on, think about the possible goals for Brianna in music therapy.

Possible goals and objectives

Goal: To provide support and relief for Brianna's state anxiety symptoms through music experiences.

Rationale: The oncology department has a clear scope of practice, and Carl has a deep understanding of the needs of patients in this context. Carl's knowledge and practice wisdom mean he already has a good sense of the type of goals he can reasonably set that will most likely lead to good outcomes for patients. Alongside this, his comfort with flexibility and engaging in a dynamic process may mean that identifying an overarching goal for a client is enough to guide the work. Therefore, Carl may simply document a broad goal and wait to document objectives as they unfold in each session with Brianna. Carl would likely be expected to document this goal and the emerging objectives in the recommended hospital format or procedural guidelines.

Alignments and tensions for Carl, Brianna, and the hospital

The various elements of the client-in-context theory were well aligned in this example, and so the therapeutic focus would be expected to meet the hospital culture. The high level of professional respect Carl has among his colleagues should make it relatively easy for him to work with broad goals that address patients' symptoms, while also remaining free to go in a different direction in collaboration with the patient. Carl would need to continue to foster good working relationships with his colleagues to ensure they understood and supported his empathic and dynamic process with patients. Carl's ability to move flexibly between predetermined and emerging needs, and the team's acceptance of this dynamic process, is key to the harmonious nature of this example.

APPLYING THEORY TO PRACTICE: DISCORDANT ATTRIBUTES AND FEATURES

The most challenging situations for therapists to navigate are when there are tensions between any of the players within this system. In the example below, I highlight some common tensions that might arise in practice and consider the flow-on impacts for identifying the therapeutic focus and goals.

Example: Phoebe, a music therapist working in adult disability services

In this example, I provide a hypothetical composite case of a music therapist working as a casual employee providing music therapy at an adult disability service. The section below provides a summary of the attributes and features of each player and their intersections.

Therapist's attributes. Phoebe is a new graduate who is committed to equity and justice in her work as a music therapist (values and beliefs). She subscribes to many blogs and social media groups for people with lived experience of disability (knowledge base) and has come to believe that eliminating disability traits simply to promote typical appearance is unethical (ethics of practice). Phoebe is deepening her understanding of critical disability theories and disability advocacy (theoretical framework) and wants to promote her music therapy practice as a way to build the confidence and strengths of disabled people (advocacy for profession). Within music therapy sessions, Phoebe strives to follow the lead of the person she is working with and respects their preferences for engagement in music (comfort with flexibility).

Client's attributes. Jamie is 22 years old and has a moderate intellectual disability and mild cerebral palsy. Jamie likes to be active but has difficulty walking long distances, running, and jumping (health complexity). People who don't know him well find Jamie's speech difficult to understand, and so he gives short answers to questions and rarely initiates conversation (communication style). If Jamie is in a group of more than three people, he finds it difficult to follow the conversation, which makes him anxious. Jamie likes to walk around if he is in a group of people and is more likely to answer questions when he is walking compared with sitting down (level of engagement). Jamie's favourite artist is P!nk, and he listens to the song 'Let's get this party started' repeatedly each day. The disability service manager refers Jamie to group music therapy so that he can learn to sit down during group activities and be introduced to new songs (referral themes). When the manager tells him he has music today, Jamie smiles and points to a picture of dancing and a picture of P!nk (understanding of music therapy).

Features of the context. The disability service offers positive behaviour support and employs various therapists to work in the program to reduce the use of restrictive interventions (scope of work). The service believes that with positive behaviour support, disabled people will have a better quality of life (philosophy and guidelines). While there are many different therapists working for the service, each team member comes in to facilitate a specialist program and communication takes place mostly via documentation and six-monthly service review meetings (team interactions). The service employs the music therapist to facilitate a group music therapy program (group or individual sessions) with funding for ten weeks from a government scheme (number of sessions funded). Phoebe's manager believes that motivating music activities can increase effective communication and foster desired behaviours that are included in each client's individual service plan (understanding of music therapy).

Therapeutic alliance (between client and therapist). As a casual employee, Phoebe has only been able to meet Jamie briefly before he attends the first group. When she says hello, Phoebe notices that Jamie is holding his communication board which has a photo of P!nk. Jamie smiles when Phoebe says that she knows some P!nk songs. In the music therapy group, there are six people. Phoebe asks Jamie if he would like to sit down, but he shakes his head while standing and sways from side to side (level of collaboration). Phoebe wonders if Jamie is self-regulating his anxiety by standing and swaying, and thinks that he seems to be enjoying listening to the songs and discussion.

Client autonomy (between the client and the context). The disability service coordinates a care team for each client. Each care team meets six-monthly to identify goals and plan services, and Jamie attends these meetings too. Jamie has been able to identify services he wants to receive, such as music therapy, and hopes that he can have a job one day in the community. Jamie's care team explains that sitting at a table with other people might help him to get a job and writes this as one of his goals.

Professional compatibility (between the therapist and the context). As a casual employee, Phoebe is not able to attend many of the care team meetings (team collaboration). She notices that music therapy is often described as an 'activity' in service plans and has tried to explain that she values working in a relationship-based and person-centred way. Phoebe reads Jamie's goal to sit down during group sessions and respects that the care team is trying to improve his future job opportunities. However, she feels uncomfortable doing any more than inviting Jamie to sit down during the music therapy group. When Phoebe explains to the service manager that Jamie seems to be standing up to self-regulate his social anxiety, and therefore the goal is normocentric,[1] the manager seems irritated (respect). The manager tells Phoebe that their

---

[1] Normocentric is the view that disability-related traits are often stigmatized (i.e. considered abnormal) even when they have an adaptive function and are not harmful. More information is available from articles by scholars with lived experience of disability (Ne'eman, 2021; Mottron, 2017).

funding is for positive behaviour support, and so perhaps she can encourage Jamie to sit down by rewarding him with his favourite P!nk song. Phoebe replies by stating that 'expression of identity' and 'expanding ways to regulate emotions' would be more suitable goals for Jamie in music therapy. Phoebe also explains that she prefers to go with the flow of sessions and create opportunities for collaboration with clients.

> Before reading on, consider what you would do in Phoebe's situation. How might Phoebe reconcile the tensions about the therapeutic focus of the music therapy sessions?

Possible goals and objectives

This is a challenging scenario that highlights the tensions that can exist when the agendas of each player engaged in the goals process do not align. The collaboration and respect within the team are limited, leading to a poor fit between the music therapist's philosophy and the context's scope of practice. The care team has already articulated the broad goals for the service, yet the music therapist disagrees that these goals are appropriate for Jamie in the context of music therapy. While Jamie has been included in service planning discussions, the organization's scope of practice defines most of the parameters of service possibilities.

In supervision, Phoebe could use the client-in-context theory to help her map out the various attributes and features impacting the process. Phoebe might benefit from deeply considering her practice ethics and the possibilities for advocating for clients accessing services from this organization. By reflecting on the situation, Phoebe should strive to find a way forward that avoids the pitfalls of simply fitting in with the demands of the context or working on covert goals in the music therapy group that are not articulated in Jamie's care plan.

In the section below, I imagine one possible outcome following Phoebe's deep reflection. This is by no means the only possibility. Any therapist in Phoebe's situation will benefit from supervision and support to navigate this challenging scenario.

Now that she has more clarity about the situation, Phoebe arranges to meet with the service manager. Phoebe explains that she is uncomfortable using Jamie's favourite song as a reward for sitting down and that this approach may increase his anxiety. Further, Phoebe explains that there is no guarantee that approaching the goal of sitting down in this way will lead to generalized behaviour in Jamie's future employment context. Phoebe instead proposes that the music therapy group can focus on experiencing different ways to manage anxiety. She explains that the group can be encouraged to try a variety of music-based strategies that involve different body positions like standing, moving, and sitting, such as movement to music, breathing/singing, instrument playing, and music listening. Phoebe further advocates for Jamie by suggesting that his walking and standing behaviours could be explained to future employers, and that Jamie might be able to contribute to an introduction letter about himself that is provided to work colleagues. The manager sets up a care team meeting and invites Phoebe to discuss her ideas with the full team, including Jamie. At the end of the meeting, the following goal is collaboratively determined:

Goal: For Jamie to experience a range of music-based strategies to support relaxation and emotional regulation in the music therapy group sessions.

APPLYING THEORY TO PRACTICE:
GETTING STARTED IN REAL LIFE

In the sections above, I worked through hypothetical scenarios with either somewhat harmonious alignments between the players or somewhat discordant alignments. In each scenario, you could imagine the music therapist mapping out their understanding of the system to help them to identify possibilities for the therapeutic focus and the goals. Therapists should not expect there to be a single correct direction to proceed in, as a theory can only scaffold thought and discussion. I am also not proposing that this theory must be followed each and every time a goal needs to be written. As the research participants highlighted, their knowledge built over time and certain aspects of goal writing eventually became second nature to them and therefore did not always need deep contemplation.

When an aspect of our practice feels uneasy, it is valuable to pause and reflect. In many ways, the contexts in which we live can be fundamentally oppressive, both for therapists and the people we work with. Deep-seated injustices and inequities resulting from racism, ableism, colonialism, sexism, and classism create privilege for some and oppress many (Baines, 2012, 2021). While the client-in-context theory invites therapists to reflect on the features of the context and the flow-on impact for their practice, I am in no way advocating that we must appease systems that are built on injustice and inequity. As therapists, I believe we have an ethical responsibility to work towards social justice and emancipation, and actively resist colluding with the system by working on goals that require clients to accept oppressive policies and practices.

For novice therapists, early-career therapists, or therapists commencing work in a new context, engaging with this theory as a reflexive tool may help them to identify salient attributes and features that are likely to impact their work. Mapping out the system may help therapists to have better conversations with clients, families, managers, and supervisors. They might gain clarity about their own practice philosophy and possible reasons for any tensions they experience in relation to the people they work with and team members.

For more experienced therapists, practice wisdom and confidence to explore topics in supervision will provide great support. However, there are circumstances where the therapist can feel unsure, confused, or in conflict with the system. The client-in-context theory can be used as a reflexive tool to help scaffold the process prior to or in lieu of supervision discussions. The theory can be seen as a framework for clinical reasoning that supports practitioners to articulate their practice wisdom or tacit knowledge.

For supervisors, asking the supervisee to map out their understanding of the system might help them to stay curious in the conversation and ensure they have a fuller understanding of the tensions faced by the supervisee. The supervisee can be asked to complete this reflection before the meeting, or aspects of the theory can be included in the reflexive discussions.

This theory can therefore be used as a prism for engaging in ongoing reflexive practice, as a precursor to a supervision discussion, or within supervision, to unravel personal perceptions of each attribute. In a similar approach to the way I articulated the hypothetical scenarios above, therapists can reflect on prompts based on each of the attributes. In the box below, I have provided some examples of prompt questions. Corresponding worksheets 1–5 are available in the Appendix to support therapists to document their reflexive process.

Therapist's attributes

- Values and beliefs:
  - How do you define your music therapy practice?
  - How would you describe your practice values?
- Theoretical framework:
  - What theories inform your practice with this person or more generally?
  - Do these theories lead to overarching goals or approaches to practice?
- Knowledge base:
  - Thinking about the person you are working with, what are the common needs of people with this condition or who are in this circumstance?
  - How do you think music therapy can best help this person? What does the literature suggest?
- Ethics of practice:
  - What is your responsibility in the therapeutic relationship with this person?
  - What is important to consider about collaboration or negotiation with the person you are working with?
- Advocacy for the music therapy profession:
  - How well does the person you are working with (or the team) understand the possibilities for music therapy in this context?
  - What would you like the person you are working with (or the team) to better understand about music therapy practice?
- Comfort with flexibility:
  - How thoroughly do you plan out the session or experiences you offer to the person you are working with?
  - How appropriate do you think it is to change the goal/focus of the session at any moment?

Client's attributes

- Referral themes:
  - What are the reasons for referral to music therapy, and who has communicated these reasons to you?
  - How much involvement has the person you will work with had in expressing the reasons for referral?
- Communication style:
  - How does the person prefer to communicate?
  - How well do you need to know the person in order to understand their forms of communication?
- Level of engagement:
  - How motivated is the person to engage in a therapeutic process?
  - How motivated is the person to engage in music experiences?
  - What types of music-based or other experiences seem to engage the person best?
- Health complexity:
  - Does the person have broader health and wellbeing needs than those identified in the referral process?
  - How do the person's social and political identities intersect, and what privileges or discriminations might converge and impact the person's health and wellbeing?
- Understanding of music therapy:
  - How well does the person understand the health and wellbeing opportunities within music experiences?
  - What does the person want to do when they are in the music therapy session?
  - How well does the person understand your role as a therapist?

Features of the context

- Philosophy and guidelines:
  - What is the philosophy of the organization you work for?
  - What, if any, are the guidelines for service provision in this organization?
- Scope of work:
  - What is the organization's focus for services provided?
  - How much flexibility is possible in the delivery of therapy services?
- Number of sessions funded:
  - How does the organization determine the number of sessions that can be provided?
  - How much control is given to clients and/or therapists to determine the number of sessions?
- Group or individual sessions:
  - What is the organization's stance on providing group or individual sessions?
  - How much control is given to clients and/or therapists to determine whether group or individual sessions can be offered?
- Understanding of music therapy:
  - What might your colleagues say when asked 'How does music help?' in this context?
- Team interactions:
  - What is the team model in this context (e.g. multidisciplinary, interdisciplinary, transdisciplinary)?
  - How closely do you work with colleagues in this organization?

Therapeutic alliance (between client and therapist)

- Level of collaboration:
  - To what degree could the person you are working with collaborate with you about the focus of their music therapy?
  - How would the person you are working with indicate their willingness to engage in a particular music experience?
  - How can you best build a relationship with this person?
  - Are family members also involved in the music therapy sessions, and if so, in what way?

Client autonomy (between the client and the context)

- In what ways can the person you are working with influence the direction or focus of their music therapy sessions?
  - To what degree can the person decline participation in music therapy?

Professional compatibility (between the therapist and the context)

- Team collaboration:
  - To what degree do you think your practice values align with the organization's philosophy?
  - How well do different colleagues understand each other's role and knowledge?
- Respect:
  - To what degree do your colleagues understand the distinct benefits of music-based experiences?
  - To what degree do your colleagues value music-based forms of expression?
  - To what degree do your colleagues value engagement in creative experiences?

In the next and final chapter, I provide guidance for the technical skills of goal writing. This guidance is based on my own practice wisdom, my learnings from teaching and supervision, and my interpretations of selected pieces of literature. As will be explored, each workplace will have their own preferences for the way goals and objectives need to be structured, and therefore therapists must be responsive to their context while mindful of their ethical responsibility to the people they work with.

REFERENCES

Aigen, K. (2014). *The Study of Music Therapy: Current Issues and Concepts.* London and New York, NY: Routledge.

American Music Therapy Association. (2005). What is music therapy? Accessed on 4/11/2021 at www.musictherapy.org/about/musictherapy

Australian Music Therapy Association. (2021). What is music therapy? Accessed on 12/11/2021 at www.austmta.org.au/about-us/what-is-mt

Baines, S. (2012). Music therapy as an anti-oppressive practice. *The Arts in Psychotherapy 40*(1), 1–5. Accessed on 3/11/2021 at https://doi.org/10.1016/j.aip.2012.09.003

Baines, S. (2021). Anti-oppressive music therapy: Updates and future considerations. *The Arts in Psychotherapy 75*, 1–5. Accessed on 3/11/2021 at https://doi.org/10.1016/j.aip.2021.101828

Dey, I. (2007). Grounding Categories. In A. Bryant & K. Charmaz (eds) *The SAGE Handbook of Grounded Theory*. London: SAGE Publications.

Ghetti, C. (2015). Maintaining the dialogue of influence: Developing music therapy theory in pace with practice and research. *Approaches: Music Therapy & Special Music Education*, Special Issue 7(1), 30–37.

Mottron, L. (2017). Should we change targets and methods of early intervention in autism, in favor of a strengths-based education? *European Child & Adolescent Psychiatry 26*(7), 815–825. Accessed on 4/11/2021 at https://doi.org/10.1007/s00787-017-0955-5

Ne'eman, A. (2021). When disability is defined by behavior, outcome measures should not promote 'passing'. *AMA Journal of Ethics 23*(7), 569–575. Accessed on 4/11/2021 at https://doi.org/10.1001/amajethics.2021.569

Stige, B. (2015). The practice turn in music therapy theory. *Music Therapy Perspectives 33*(1), 3–11. Accessed on 4/11/2021 at https://doi.org/https://doi.org/10.1093/mtp/miu050

Strauss, A.L. & Corbin, J. (1998). *Basics of Qualitative Research: Techniques and Procedures for Developing Grounded Theory* (2nd edn). Thousand Oaks, CA: SAGE.

Thompson, G.A. (2020). A grounded theory of music therapists' approach to goal processes within their clinical practice. *The Arts in Psychotherapy 70*. Accessed on 3/11/2021 at https://doi.org/10.1016/j.aip.2020.101680

CHAPTER 9

Considerations for goal writing

The client-in-context theory does not provide guidance to support the technical skill of goal writing. During the research interviews that informed this theory, I invited participants to describe what they considered to be the essential elements of goal processes in music therapy. Goal processes include the behaviours associated with goals (Cooper & Law, 2018), and so I expected the participants to offer some rules, guidelines, or protocols for how to write goals based on what they have taught their own students or discussed in supervision. However, very few participants offered clear suggestions. Instead, they focused on the conditions leading to and surrounding goal processes, and highlighted that the context for the work is the key driver for how the goal will be written or expressed.

Therefore, I believe there is no single way to write a goal, and it may not even be possible to say there is a right way at all. Perhaps the most that can be said is that there are more or less *better* ways to write a goal *for use in a particular context at a particular time for a particular purpose*. In this chapter, I provide a set of considerations that are a synthesis of my own practice wisdom, my learnings from teaching and supervision, and my understandings of selected pieces of literature. Each reader will need to determine which elements from these considerations are most applicable to their situation.

ACKNOWLEDGING THE IMPACT OF TERMINOLOGY

The terms we use to describe our work are powerful and carry with them different connotations depending on a person's life experience. For example, in everyday life the word 'goal' can bring to mind sporting metaphors that imply a sense of winning or losing, success or failure. Terms such as 'aim', 'journey', or 'plan' might be preferred by some people as they infer a more open approach (Cooper & Law, 2018). When we talk about evaluating therapy goals, using terms like 'target behaviour' and 'criteria for success' might create anxiety in the people we work with and feel poorly aligned with strengths-based and collaborative approaches (Molyneux *et al.*, 2012).

Goals can have a variety of purposes: they can provide a helpful focus for the therapeutic experiences (Cooper & Law, 2018), or they might be constructed to enable objective measurement of progress (Carpente, 2018; Hanser, 2018). Despite the different connotations that various terms might suggest, the language of 'goals' and 'objectives' are widely adopted in many professional music therapy communities (Abbott, 2020). Goals are generally understood to be broad statements of desired change, while objectives are more specific and tend to be short-term in nature (Gfeller & Davis, 2008). Objectives are often written to provide more precision regarding the aspects that will indicate whether a goal has been achieved (Polen *et al.*, 2017).

While widely used, it is worth acknowledging that the terms 'goals' and 'objectives' are part of therapists' professional jargon and may be confronting for some clients. The consensus term I coined for the client-in-context theory was 'therapeutic focus' since this has broader application to various practice settings. To ask an individual, group, or family 'What would you like to focus on in music therapy?' feels quite different from 'What is your goal in music therapy?' The statements that can be developed following this discussion could take various forms.

A complementary consideration for use of terminology is the grammatical structure of the statement itself. There are various ways that statements can be expressed, including:

- **Person-centred statements** (Abbott, 2020; Carpente, 2018; Polen *et al.*, 2017). These statements clearly articulate the change, growth, or focus of therapy for the individual or group, such as 'For Sam to...', or 'Sam will...', or 'For the group to...', or 'The group will...' Some individuals may also prefer to be more straightforward in their expression, such as 'I want to be able to...' or 'I want my family member to...' Respecting the preferred expression of each person is an important factor in building the therapeutic alliance.
- **Purpose statements** (Polen *et al.*, 2017). These statements identify a broad area of need, such as 'foster creative expression', 'share musical attention', or 'expand social communication repertoire'.
- **Therapist-centred statements** (Abbott, 2020). These statements articulate the therapist's intention during music therapy sessions, such as 'Provide opportunities for creative expression through musical improvisation'.

Beyond these broad grammatical considerations, goal statements can then be more specifically constructed using various structural components. Elaine Abbott's (2020) research with 457 board-certified music therapists in the United States revealed 15 possible components making up goals and objectives, including: 'client, service provider, task, area of need, problem, direction of change, client mechanism, condition, treatment continuation or frequency, level of support, measurement, measurement tool, purpose for treatment, music therapist's role, and timeframe' (p.180). Abbott's analysis showed that goals typically included only two or three of these components (area of need, direction of change, and/or client), while objectives typically included three to five components (client, task, measurement(s), level of support, and/or condition). For both goals and objectives, the maximum number of components therapists included in their statements was seven. These findings further support the fact that there is no single template for writing goals and objectives in practice.

FORMATS THAT ARE BETTER SUITED TO TRACKING OBSERVABLE CHANGE

In some contexts, it is necessary for goals and objectives to provide a clear means to track change and measure progress in therapy. Goals and objectives that need to meet this evaluative purpose must be constructed in a way that makes it possible to measure the expected outcome, target behaviour, or variable of change (Carpente, 2018). Therefore, focusing on outcomes that can be measured will have flow-on impacts on the music experiences that are offered and the way they are facilitated. It is important for music therapists to reflect on whether goal statements *need* to be constructed in this way, since they are not the only option. Goal statements can become powerful drivers of the therapy experience, and therefore serious consideration should be given to deeper questions around the meaningfulness of the goal, since focusing on an outcome that can be measured can limit the scope of music therapy practice.

In order to track observable change, Suzanne Hanser (2018) specifies that the goal must include a clear description of a target response and that a 'complete behavioural description or response definition' (p.137) must accompany the goal to ensure that outcomes will be valid and credible. Hanser proposes that objectives should be written using the SMART format to ensure all essential aspects of evaluation criteria are included, and the focus is appropriate for the client. The SMART format includes the following aspects:

- **S**pecific: concrete and specific detail of target response.
- **M**easurable: target response can be quantified numerically.
- **A**chievable: feasible for the client in relation to their assessment.
- **R**ealistic: target response is appropriate for music therapy and the client.
- **T**ime frame: the expected time it should take for the target response to be achieved.

The following example is taken from Hanser's *The New Music Therapist's Handbook* (2018, p.142):

Goal: To increase awareness of others.

Target response: Visual focusing on object or person (a detailed definition must be provided of this target response).

Objective: To maintain visual focus (as defined) on a musical instrument or sound source as it is moved six inches in five different directions.

Hanser's example leaves the 'time frame' aspect out of the objective and suggests that a date can be set for review of progress as an alternative.

John Carpente (2018) proposes a format for ensuring that goals are constructed to be 'concrete and measurable' (p.3) based on goal attainment scaling (GAS) guidelines. Once a variable of change is identified, the GAS method requires therapists to 'scale' the client's performance from the worst to the best outcome. Further, the therapist's responsibility to provide opportunities for the client to demonstrate their progress is essential within the construction of the goals and the implementation of therapy. The following example is taken from Carpente's 2018 publication, where the expected level of the goal is written as follows:

Goal: The client will shift musical attention from basic beating on the drum to punctuating the end of a musical phrase with the cymbal in 60% of the opportunities provided by the therapist. (p.4)

The frequency of response is scaled from least favourable (responding to 20% of the opportunities) to most favourable (responding to 100% of the opportunities). There are many elements of the SMART format in Carpente's approach to the GAS method. However, in this method, the goal is not just described as achieved or unachieved, as progress can be tracked with more nuance.

It is important to reiterate that the *person-in-context* must be considered, since goals constructed in this way will drive the facilitation of music experiences. For some therapists in certain contexts working with particular people, these goal statements will feel like a good fit. For other therapists working in different circumstances, these goal statements will feel like a poor fit and other possibilities should be considered.

FORMATS THAT ARE BETTER SUITED TO SCAFFOLDING A JOURNEY OF GROWTH

In some contexts, goal statements are used to provide a focus and direction for the therapeutic work and allow for more subjective forms of appraisal or reflection. The focus of the therapeutic work may not lend itself to being operationally or concretely described. The notion of improvement or progress may be uncertain or irrelevant, and so concepts such as flourishing, expansion, or evolution may be a better fit. Nonetheless, there will be a therapeutic focus for the work that can be meaningfully communicated for the person-in-context.

In these circumstances, the goal statement needs to provide 'good enough' parameters to support practice and the therapeutic alliance. When writing goal statements to scaffold practice in this broader sense, simply including components related to the area of need, or the direction of change, has recently been described in the research literature (Abbott, 2020). The box below provides my synthesis of components that may be useful to include in broad goal statements that are intended to scaffold the therapeutic process and provide a focus for the client and therapist.

Suggested components for creating broad goal statements

1. Express the goal using person-first language, such as 'For Alice to...' or 'For the group to...' The statement could be in first-person where appropriate, such as 'I would like to...' or 'I would like my family member to...'
2. Include a description of change, if warranted. This description does not need to be expressed in terms of increasing or decreasing. Other possibilities include: extend, expand, deepen, experience.
3. Include the area of need. It is helpful to ensure that the statement has only one area of need. If there are two areas of need, then it is advised to create two goal statements.
4. Include the music therapy method or music experience. For goals, the music method would be broadly described. For objectives, the music method could be described more specifically.

Based on the suggested components above, I have created two different examples as follows:

Example 1: Including all four components

Alice will expand her repertoire of musical ideas initiated within free improvisation with the music therapist.

Breakdown of components:

- Alice will [person-first language]
- Expand [description of change]
- Her repertoire of musical ideas initiated [area of need]
- Within free improvisation with the music therapist [distinct music therapy method – broadly described for a goal]

Example 2: Including three components

Alice will initiate musical ideas within free improvisation with the music therapist.

Breakdown of components:

- Alice will [person-first language]
- Initiate musical ideas [area of need]
- Within free improvisation with the music therapist [distinct music therapy method – broadly described for a goal]

Having traversed a wide territory related to goal processes in music therapy, it is important to acknowledge that the content of the goals themselves have not been directly addressed. This is because the goal process sits within the larger process of therapy, which includes the way referrals take place, the way the therapist and client get to know each other (assessment), and the ways that the work will need to be documented and evaluated. To conclude, the box below presents considerations for how to critically reflect on the goal that has been identified and make any further adjustments or refinements.

Critically reflecting on the goal statement

Is the goal or objective:

- Meaningful to client. Do the client and the team/ organization agree that this goal is useful?
- Feasible. Are the client's health and current abilities a good match for the goal?
- Suitable for music therapy. Can music therapy offer something distinct in working with this goal? Is there literature to support the use of music therapy in this area of need? Do the music therapy methods align with the interests of the client?
- Able to be evaluated in a suitable way. Will the achievements, progress, or experiences be docu- mented? What options for evaluation are meaningful for the client and the team/organization – for example, observation, client report, team report, musical analysis, therapist reflection, standardized assessment?
- Fixed or flexible. Does the context require predeter- mined goals? Are here-and-now, collaborative, or flexible goals possible or desirable in the context?

Throughout this book, my contention has been that goal processes are a central part of broader therapy processes. Therapy must always have a purpose, and therapists have an ethical responsibility to part- ner with the people they work with to find the most meaningful therapeutic focus to meet their current needs and aspirations. Goal statements are powerful and can both consciously and unconsciously drive practice. Engaging in reflexivity throughout the goal process may support therapists to achieve a more compassionate and ethical focus on the person-in-context.

REFERENCES

Abbott, E.A. (2020). Music therapists' goal and objective writing practices. *Music Therapy Perspectives 38*(2), 178–186. Accessed on 3/11/2021 at https://doi.org/10.1093/mtp/miz018

Carpente, J.A. (2018). Goal attainment scaling: A method for evaluating progress toward developmentally based music-centered treatment goals for children with autism spectrum disorder. *Music Therapy Perspectives 36*(2), 215–223. Accessed on 3/11/2021 at https://doi.org/https://doi.org/10.1093/mtp/mix021

Cooper, M. & Law, D. (2018). Introduction. In M. Cooper & D. Law (eds) *Working with Goals in Psychotherapy and Counselling.* Oxford: Oxford University Press.

Gfeller, K.E. & Davis, W.B. (2008). The Music Therapy Treatment Process. In W.B. Davis, K.E. Gfeller & M.H. Thaut (eds) *An Introduction to Music Therapy Theory and Practice.* Silver Spring, MD: American Music Therapy Association.

Hanser, S.B. (2018). *The New Music Therapist's Handbook* (3rd edn). Boston, MA: Berklee Press.

Molyneux, C., Koo, N.-H., Piggot-Irvine, E., Talmage, A., Travaglia, R. & Willis, M. (2012). Doing it together: Collaborative research on goal-setting and review in a music therapy centre. *New Zealand Journal of Music Therapy 10*, 6–38.

Polen, D.W., Shultis, C.L. & Wheeler, B. (2017). *Clinical Training Guide for the Student Music Therapist* (2nd edn). New Braunfels, TX: Barcelona Publishers.

Appendix: Worksheets

The following worksheets are available to download from www.jkp.com/catalogue/book/9781787756083 for your own personal use.

WORKSHEET 1: THE THERAPIST'S ATTRIBUTES

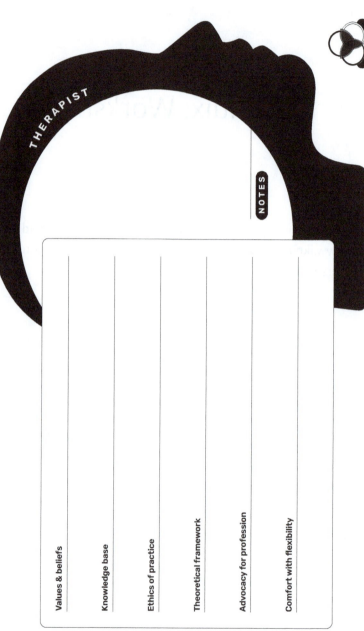

Values & beliefs

Knowledge base

Ethics of practice

Theoretical framework

Advocacy for profession

Comfort with flexibility

WORKSHEET 2: THE CLIENT'S ATTRIBUTES

CLIENT

NOTES

Referral themes

Communication style

Level of engagement

Health complexity

Understanding of music therapy

WORKSHEET 3: FEATURES OF THE CONTEXT

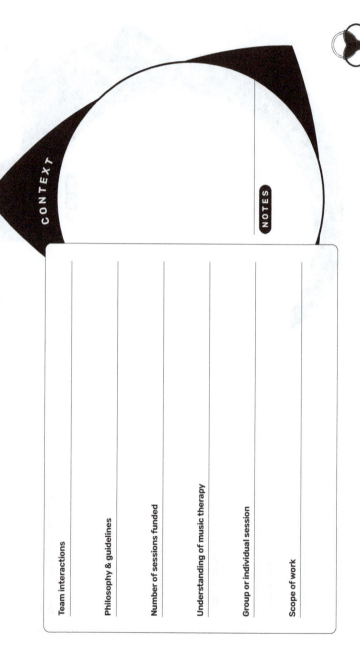

CONTEXT

NOTES

Team interactions

Philosophy & guidelines

Number of sessions funded

Understanding of music therapy

Group or individual session

Scope of work

WORKSHEET 4: INTERSECTIONS BETWEEN THE PLAYERS

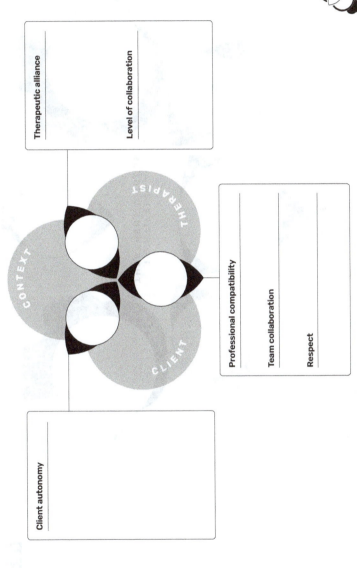

Therapeutic alliance

Level of collaboration

Client autonomy

Professional compatibility

Team collaboration

Respect

CONTEXT

THERAPIST

CLIENT

WORKSHEET 5: MAPPING THE FULL THEORY

THERAPIST

PROFESSIONAL COMPATIBILITY

CONTEXT

IDENTIFYING A THERAPEUTIC FOCUS

THERAPEUTIC ALLIANCE

CLIENT AUTONOMY

CLIENT

NOTES

CLIENT-NEEDS CHANGING OVER TIME — THERAPY PROCESS

Index